T0182481

SHAWN GOODMAN

HOW TO SURVIVE YOUR PARENTS

A TEEN'S GUIDE TO THRIVING IN A DIFFICULT FAMILY

 ROCKY POND BOOKS

ROCKY POND BOOKS
An imprint of Penguin Random House LLC
1745 Broadway, New York, New York 10019

Ⓟ

First published in the United States of America by Rocky Pond Books,
an imprint of Penguin Random House LLC, 2024
Copyright © 2024 by Shawn Goodman

Penguin supports copyright. Copyright fuels creativity, encourages diverse
voices, promotes free speech, and creates a vibrant culture. Thank you for
buying an authorized edition of this book and for complying with copyright
laws by not reproducing, scanning, or distributing any part of it in any form
without permission. You are supporting writers and allowing Penguin to
continue to publish books for every reader.

Rocky Pond Books is a registered trademark and the colophon is a
trademark of Penguin Random House LLC.
The Penguin colophon is a registered trademark of Penguin Books Limited.

Visit us online at PenguinRandomHouse.com.

Library of Congress Cataloging-in-Publication Data is available.

ISBN 9780593697528

1 3 5 7 9 10 8 6 4 2

Printed in the United States of America

BVG

Design by Jason Henry | Text set in Arvo

This is a work of nonfiction.
Some names and identifying details have been changed.

CONTENTS

WHO IS THIS BOOK FOR?

It may seem obvious, but *How to Survive Your Parents* was written for you and not your parents. If your parents want to read and learn more about you, that's great, but they should get a different book. There are dozens of good ones out there.

And if they're worried about what you might learn in these pages, they should relax. Seriously! I'm not going to disclose any parenting trade secrets—and I can tell you with certainty that there aren't any. I'm not going to equip you with manipulative superpowers either. Sorry, but those don't exist.

What I *am* going to do is guide you to understand and improve one of the most important relationships in your life: the one that exists between you and your parents. This doesn't mean you're going to become best friends and enjoy beautiful Hallmark moments together. It could happen, but that's not the goal here. The goal is to help you learn the skills needed to change how you and your parents see each other. You will talk more and argue less. You will stop clinging to resentments and rehashing old hurts. Most importantly, you will begin to see each other as separate and authentic people.

It's possible that you might be reluctant to go forward because of what reading a book like this could mean—that your family problems are real and not going away. That your parents aren't the people you want them to be. That your life isn't either. It's okay to feel that way. You're in the right place. There's a reason you found this book. Or maybe a reason the book found you.

BEFORE WE BEGIN

I want this book to be honest. It needs to be, because it takes too much courage for a person your age to stand up and say: "I'm hurting, and I want to try and make my life better." The least I can do is summon my own courage and be honest with you, the reader, about these three questions:

Who am I?

Why am I writing this book?

Why should you take the time to read it?

Here goes.

First answer: At the time of writing, I'm a fifty-two-year-old married white guy with two kids (one finishing high school, one finishing college), a big gentle dog, and a fierce and discourteous cat. I live in your average vinyl-sided ranch in Upstate New York, where I work as a psychologist at a big high school. For fun, I coach Special Olympics athletes, tinker with bikes, and play in an old-guy soccer league. I also write YA novels that focus on mental health, second chances, and the power of relationships. If this sounds overly cheerful and rehearsed, know that it's almost impossible to make it to my age without brushing up against things like grief, despair, addiction, and even suicide.

But surviving bad things isn't a good enough qualification for writing this particular book, so I'll share an early story. I was fifteen when my mother and father started having marriage problems. One of them pulled me aside to vent about the other. But the venting wasn't *just* venting. It was an attempt to see if I agreed that the other parent was being unreasonable, or was in the wrong. I remember being confused at first, wondering why these people who were supposed to be competent adults were acting so badly. And then it hit me: They didn't know how to handle their problems.

To fifteen-year-old me, this was nothing short of a revelation. My parents weren't trying to act like assholes. They didn't intend to put their problems on me or make our home tense and unlivable. They were desperate! They were intelligent and decent human beings but hadn't a clue how to manage that particular stage of their relationship. And here's the important part: The pain of it was driving them to act badly, and their acting badly was driving a wedge between us.

You're probably thinking, "Yeah, so what? I've been through way worse," or "I know kids whose family problems are much bigger." I know those kids too, and I agree. I'm sharing this story because the ordinary situation of my parents' marriage problems led me to see that my parents didn't know what the hell they were doing. They weren't any better equipped to handle the stresses of life than anyone else. And *anyone else* included me! That was the big realization.

In that moment, a shift occurred in which I started to see my parents differently. They went from being my mother and father to a couple of people who were struggling. Individuals who had gotten far enough in life to have a marriage, kids, careers, and a house, but didn't know what to do next. It's incredibly common stuff, I know. But here's the really interesting part: What followed was not a surge of empathy or understanding from me. It was anger!

I was angry that one of the core rules of life—as I understood it—had been broken. Parents were supposed to have their shit together, and mine didn't. Parents were supposed to be there for their kids. Mine weren't. Because of this, I was going to have to rely on myself more. Sure, I'd still need plenty of help and support from them, especially around the basics of food, clothing, money, and transportation. But with the big things like figuring out relationships and finding meaning, I was quite likely on my own. This was a scary thought, but it was also exciting. I felt the burden of responsibility, but also the possibility of freedom. And it has taken the last thirty-seven years to begin to understand the connection between those two things. Freedom and responsibility. We're going to explore that connection in this book, but don't worry: It's not going to take you nearly as long to figure it out, and you don't have to become a psychologist to do so.

Second answer: I was inspired to write this book

by teens I've met and talked with across the country, in places like New York, California, Massachusetts, and Pennsylvania. Some of these teens were from wealthy families, while others lived in public housing. Some were dedicated students and athletes, while many preferred to play video games, read fantasy novels, or hang out with friends. Most were sad and lonely. No matter the differences of money, status, or lifestyle, many of the teens I've known had one thing in common: They felt disconnected from their parents and wanted to get along better with them. They wanted to feel more warmth and love in that relationship. Even those who had experienced years of abuse and neglect! They still wanted to be close to their parents and feel like they belonged.

Maybe this shouldn't surprise me. These are the things everyone wants.

It's what I want too—for myself, my children, and the teens I get to know at work. As a parent, I've made more mistakes than I can count. I'm still making them, but I keep trying to learn and grow. It's the same at work, repeated over the span of thousands of teens and their families with that one constant: Teens want to get along better with their parents.

They might come into my office asking for help with attention, mood, grades, or other life problems. Eventually, though, they talk about what's really troubling them. It's home.

Specifically, their relationships with their parents.

The feeling that they don't belong and maybe never will.

I don't need to describe how painful these feelings are. You probably know firsthand.

Third answer: Why should you bother reading this book? Let me start by saying I don't possess any secret knowledge, quick fixes, or easy answers—and I'm increasingly suspicious of anyone who claims that they do. I'm also suspicious of books with specific steps or plans that you need to follow to see results. Why? Because everyone is unique. You're unique. Your parents are unique. And so is your relationship with them. What I'm going to talk about instead of steps and plans are the most important things I've learned from my work with teens and parents, and from my experience of raising my own teens. It's an understatement to say that it has been an adventure, and I am excited to share it with you.

WHAT I KNOW

YOUR PAIN IS VALID.

The pain you've experienced from your struggles at home is 100 percent valid. It's not a phase you will outgrow. It's not teen angst, or moodiness, or out-of-control hormones, or fallout from being led astray by bad friends. It's not *just in your head*. It's not a case of you being too sensitive, weak, or dramatic. You're not blowing things out of proportion. Your pain is real and valid.

Why do parents discredit your feelings? Because all of the incorrect explanations above are cliches that have been accepted in our culture. And cliches are always easier to accept than the truth. Or maybe adults were told the exact same things by their parents when they were your age. Maybe they were given bad advice by friends, family, or so-called experts. But regardless of the reasons, and no matter what your parents may have said, your feelings are totally legitimate.

PERFECT DOESN'T EXIST.

There's no such thing as a perfect parent, perfect kid, or perfect family. There are, however, plenty that look perfect. The illusion of perfection is so convincing that we end up living in a state of constant comparison where we always fall short. Each repetition of this leaves us feeling less worthy. It's a terrible trick.

I know it's a trick because the teens I work with tell me in exquisite detail about the lives of these allegedly perfect families. They live in beautiful homes in the best neighborhoods. The parents have prestigious jobs. They take vacations to exotic places and post lots of happy pictures where everyone seems to love one another in the deepest, truest way. The teens are the best students and athletes, belong to the right groups and clubs, and have the shiniest social lives that you can follow minute by minute on every social media app.

But what the kids who tell me these things don't realize is that these perfect teens and their parents have come to my office with the same problems. That's right: The perfect families are struggling with the same issues as everyone else. Shiny on the outside, but just as raw and unhappy on the inside.

You could take this to mean a lot of things. Here's what it means to me: Family relationships are complex and always changing. When these relationships cause you pain, it takes effort and understanding to make them better, and comparing yourself with others just gets in the way.

YOU ARE NOT YOUR PARENTS.

This may seem simple enough, but it's quite a complicated idea. Look, you and your parents may have the same last name. You may even look alike and sound alike. But you are actually separate people.

What does that mean? It means that you have the right to form your own ideas, opinions, and values. Some of your ideas, opinions, and values will clash with those of your parents, and this might be hard for them to accept. It's going to create conflict. They may pressure you to change or fall in line, and this may make you feel sad, guilty, ashamed, or angry. But whatever the situation, you can learn how to deal with this conflict more skillfully, and that can change everything.

If it sounds hard, it is. It will likely be one of the hardest things you will ever do, which might explain why so many adults are still struggling to resolve their issues from childhood. They have not done this kind of work. It also explains why families often limp along with serious—but fixable—problems for years, decades, or even generations!

But doing the hard work of changing is so worth it. The reward is that you get to live your life as a whole person. You get to love and experience joy. You get to feel what it's like to be in a relationship where both people are seen, heard, and understood. Besides, what's the alternative? To pretend to be someone you're not? To stay silent and hope things will change—or hope that *other people* will change? I don't think any of these options is acceptable. I hope you agree.

YOUR PARENTS ARE NOT YOU.

Your parents have their own lives and should not be living vicariously through you. Whatever goals and ambitions they have for themselves, they should try to achieve them directly. That's their work to do in the course of their lives. You have your own work, which you can only do if you're free to focus on yourself. This isn't selfishness or narcissism. There is plenty of space in life to focus on yourself and still care about others. There's space enough, too, to focus on yourself and be part of a family.

Nowhere is this more apparent than in school and extracurricular activities. I've known teens who were incredibly talented at sports or music but ended up hating it. Even though they were outwardly successful—winning games and awards—they were succeeding for their parents and not themselves. Most of these gifted athletes and musicians ultimately quit not because of the competition or hard work involved. They quit because it felt bad to have someone else living through them. It sucked the joy from their experiences and, ultimately, became a source of anger and resentment.

One girl, a nationally ranked runner, summed it up this way: "When my mom posts my times on social media and records video for my college highlight reel, I see that she only loves me because I win. It's the same with my coach and teammates. It feels terrible and I dream of quitting, but I'm afraid that if I do, I'll be completely alone."

YOU ARE NOT YOUR GRADES.

Competition for grades, college admissions, and other kinds of achievement is at an all-time high. There's pressure to work hard in school, get good grades, and possibly take a certain number of AP classes. You may be expected to participate in sports, join after-school clubs, hold a part-time job, and volunteer. In the spaces between these activities and pursuits, you're supposed to have a healthy, active social life.

I could go on, but you get the idea.

Does all of the above sound stressful? It is. Exhausting? Very.

Don't get me wrong. There's nothing problematic about achievement, or about pursuing your own goals. Just make sure they're *your* goals and not your parents'. And make sure that the pursuit of them doesn't take over your whole life. Most importantly, challenge the message that your worth as a person is tied to your achievement. It's not.

Quite simply, you are not your grades.

Nor are you the level of difficulty of the classes you're taking. There's no such thing as an AP person, or an Honors person. You're a person. I'm a person. We're all people.

Let's keep going with this. You are not your GPA. Or your weighted GPA. Or your class rank.

Nor are you the sum of your extracurriculars, volunteer experiences, and sports.

You are not your highest score on the ACT or SAT.

You are not the college or university you want to go to. You are not the number of colleges you apply to. You are not your first-choice school or your safety school. You are not the college or university that your parents or siblings went to, or the one your parents or siblings would like *you* to go to.

You are not your college essay, even if it really stands out and perfectly reflects your personality and values.

Are you with me so far? If so, you might be asking, "Who *am* I, then?"

You are multidimensional. You are complex and evolving. You cannot be defined by numbers, scores, levels, or acceptance rates. You will be defined instead by your experiences, and by the relationships you have with people you care about. You will be defined by your values. Your hopes and dreams. You will be defined by the things you are learning right now, and what you want to learn about in the future. You will be defined by the unique sense of meaning and purpose you are developing.

RELATIONSHIPS ARE IMPORTANT.

First, the quality of your life has a lot to do with the quality of your relationships.

This is so important that it bears repeating. The quality of your life depends on the quality of your relationships.

Second, the quality of your relationships depends on how well you're able to have difficult conversations. Which is the same as having conversations about difficult subjects. I'm not expecting you to know how to do this. Most people spend most of their lives avoiding difficult conversations. A big part of the chapters that follow is aimed at teaching you the skills needed to navigate these kinds of conversations safely. That means coming away with your dignity and self-respect intact. Staying connected to your true self.

Some people think they're having difficult conversations, but they're really just unloading their feelings without knowing what they need from the relationship. It makes for good TV drama, but in reality, it's a surefire way to blow up your relationships. The opposite, and equally ineffectual, approach is to quietly retreat and swallow your feelings. What I'm talking about instead is being honest and clear about how you feel *and* about what you need.

When you know how to do this, the world changes. No, that's not entirely true; the world stays the same, but *your relationships* change. They become stable and supportive, leading to trust and belonging. And when that happens, you can feel good about yourself and spend more of your time on what's important to you.

NOT TALKING ABOUT THE HARD STUFF DOESN'T MAKE IT GO AWAY.

Waiting to feel better doesn't work either.

Neither does waiting for other people to change.

Seriously, people have spent their whole lives waiting and hoping for their parents to change. I know people in their seventies and eighties who still talk with sadness and hurt about their relationships with their parents. They wanted it to go differently. To have felt loved. To have been treated better. Or simply to have been seen and heard. You might be thinking, "It's sad that they can never go back and change things." What's even sadder, though, is when people carry these hurts and resentments into their future relationships. But it doesn't have to be this way.

I know people in their teens and early twenties who have done what these older people never could. They have taken control of their lives and worked to improve their relationships with their parents. One very insightful eighteen-year-old told me this: "Other people see my parents as good people, and I guess they are. They're good at their jobs. They're what you'd call *good citizens*. But they're crap parents. The minute I realized this, I knew I had to be in control and make decisions for myself." Over the next few years, he effectively taught his parents how he wanted to be treated. It wasn't perfect, and there was a lot of backsliding. Two steps forward and one step back. But he said that the changes were real and made a big difference in his life. He no longer felt pushed and pulled by the forces of guilt and resentment. He started making decisions based on his own wants and needs. Most importantly, he felt closer to his parents because, through this process, they had learned to understand him better.

YOU CAN'T CHANGE ANOTHER PERSON.

And even if you *could*, I'd argue that you shouldn't. It's not your job to change them. It's theirs.

Not everyone wants to change. This may seem strange, especially when it's obvious to you and others that the person—your parent—has serious issues. They're controlling and manipulative. They argue too much. They judge and criticize others. Why wouldn't they want to change?

The reasons behind any one person's resistance to change could easily fill an entire book, or a dozen fifty-minute sessions with a really good therapist. It could be that they're narcissistic, insecure, or in denial. They may lack self-awareness or empathy. Or maybe they feel like they don't have the energy or emotional resources to change. Whatever the reason, we're not going to spend much time trying to change your parents. For one thing, it doesn't work because no one has that kind of power. And it's not your job. Your job is to focus on improving *your* life.

PEOPLE ARE REALLY BAD AT READING MINDS.

The likelihood that someone will figure out what's troubling you is very low. And the likelihood that they would actually know how to help you? I'd say that percentage is close to zero.

When we forget people are bad at reading minds, we expect them to know what we want and need. And when they don't deliver those things, we feel hurt and misunderstood. It's the same with the things that annoy and frustrate us. We end up thinking something like, "They know I can't stand it when they interrupt and talk over me. Why do they keep doing it?"

In reality, people need us to tell them what we're thinking and wanting. They also need to be told when their behavior is problematic for us. Not all the time and not in a way that is harsh or critical, but *sometimes* and in a way that is as clear and honest as it is respectful. Don't worry, we'll spend time learning about the differences between harsh/ critical and clear/direct.

LOVE ISN'T A REQUIREMENT FOR MAKING A RELATIONSHIP BETTER.

Some people struggle with relationships because they've come to believe that love is an all-or-nothing thing. You either love someone or you don't. You love them all of the time or never. You love everything about them or nothing.

The problem with this kind of thinking is it's not realistic. It might work in movies or TV shows, but the film crew has the luxury of cutting away from the dramatic scenes. What happens in between? A lot. People scroll on their phones. They have boring, meaningless conversations. They grate on each other's nerves. They say and do insensitive things and get mad at each other and argue. This is normal. It's real life.

In real life, it's possible to love certain things about a person and not others. It's possible to feel great love for someone one moment and be furious with them the next. It's possible to feel your love change over time, going up or down in intensity. Or have it change into a different kind of love. It's also possible to feel no love at all for a person and still show respect for them and occasionally enjoy their company.

SMALL CHANGES ADD UP OVER TIME.

It's hard to be patient when you're suffering, but even a 10 percent change in your relationship with your parents can make a world of difference. And a few small changes like that over a year or two? Life altering.

Here's a secret: Because small changes are often unnoticeable to other people in your family, they're less likely to react to them. And so, real change is often the cumulative effect of several small ones. In this way, your relationships can change subtly and slowly. Even without your parents noticing. You're not tripping the wires of their defenses.

YOU HAVE THE RIGHT TO BELONG IN YOUR FAMILY.

What does it mean to belong in a family? It means being seen, heard, and accepted. Your family may not treat you that way, but just know that it's still your right.

Being seen means that you don't have to hide in your room to avoid conflict or criticism. You feel comfortable being present and spending time in the common areas of your home, even if your parents are there. This doesn't mean it's always going to be fun and easy. Even in the most functional families, people argue and get on each other's nerves. They hog the remote control and talk too loud on their phones. They interrupt and say awkward things. But whatever their behavior, they shouldn't make you feel like you need to hide. They shouldn't make you feel like you aren't understood or respected.

Being seen also means that, on some level, your parents get you. They might disagree with your opinions or have totally different preferences. But they should know and acknowledge what you like and don't like. They should know what you believe in and what's important to you.

Being heard means that you have the right to share your opinion and speak up on things that matter to you. You have the right to your own opinions, even if they're different. Your parents don't have to like what you're saying or agree with it. But they should be able to listen and accept that your perspective is valid.

Being accepted is what it feels like when your parents see, hear, and understand you.

It can be experienced differently depending on who you are, but in general it's a feeling of connectedness. You know that your parents will support you through your life. They're on your side, even when they disagree. Even if they're mad at you or you're mad at them. You feel so safe, in fact, that you're no longer afraid of conflict or arguments—because the relationship is strong enough to withstand it, and both parties care enough to do the work needed.

If you're thinking, "Yeah, right!"—just wait. We'll get there.

HOW TO USE THIS BOOK

SKIP FREELY.

The structure of this book is designed to walk you through the rather complicated and scary process of working on your relationship with your parents. Each chapter will cover a different part of this process, but don't feel like you have to go in order. Everyone is different, and everyone's needs are different. A good way to start is to skim the whole book, looking at the topics and chapter headings. This will give you a preview of what's to come, and you can spend more time on what's most interesting or urgent. If something resonates strongly, start there.

DON'T READ TOO MUCH AT ANY ONE TIME.

This may sound counterintuitive, but for the kind of work you're going to be doing—intense, deep, and personal—you want to go slowly and take lots of breaks. It's not like you're studying for a test. Reading too much at one time or too quickly risks missing something important. Or it risks catching it only at a superficial level. Twenty minutes per day is a good place to start. I'd rather you read a little and think about it deeply than burn through the whole book and forget most of it.

MINIMUM EFFECTIVE DOSE

Throughout this book, we're going to focus on the smallest possible efforts that will result in the most meaningful changes. Notice I said *meaningful* and not *biggest*. Meaningful changes are those that matter to you and are doable. Small changes are easier to work into your day-to-day life. They don't require a lot of courage or a high level of risk. Nor do they require a personality transplant! For every strategy in this book, I will scale it down to the smallest and lowest-risk level for you to practice. That's the minimum effective dose.

JUDGE YOUR WORK AND INTENTIONS, NOT THE OUTCOME.

We all want results, but relationships and families are infinitely complex. And life is constantly changing and often messy. Focusing on results can undermine your work. You might be thinking, "Why bother if I can't expect to see results?" I get it, but we're not talking about financial investments or fitness goals here. If you've committed to reading this book, you've already taken an important first step. You are one of the rare people willing to take responsibility for the relationships in your life. So, give yourself credit where it's due and try to remember this when the process gets tough.

Give yourself permission to experience parts of the book emotionally.

What I mean here is, as you read, different emotions are going to come up. Some might be powerful, confusing, or scary. You might feel really angry and frustrated. Or sad. If this happens, remind yourself that it's okay to have these feelings. You're supposed to feel them. And don't worry—I'm not going to leave you hanging with intense, overwhelming emotions. At the end of the hard-work chapters, you'll find a check-in to help you process and return safely to your regular life.

EXHAUSTION CAN BE A PART OF IT.

After reading, you might find yourself feeling exhausted or wrung out. That's because this kind of work can be very taxing. Emotionally, energetically, and even physically. You might think it's no big deal to read a few pages and think a little about what's going on in your life. For some people it might *not* be a big deal. But for many, it's going to be draining. Exhaustion is one cue that it's time to slow down. Give yourself a couple of hours—or even days—and enough space to process and rest. When you feel better, go back in. If the feelings aren't going away, it might be time to talk with someone you trust or even a professional.

WRITE THINGS DOWN.

I highly recommend keeping a journal or notebook close by. Thoughts, questions, and memories will come up as you read. When this happens, set the book down, take out your journal or notebook, and write as fast and furiously as you can. The material you come up with will be really valuable. You don't want to lose it. If you're not the notebook or journal type, write directly in the margins of this book.

SHARE WITH A THERAPIST.

If you're working with a therapist or counselor, share parts of the book that are important to you. Many people feel like it's the therapist's job to figure out what their goals should be. But the more you are involved in this process, the better it will go. As a therapist myself, I love it when teens come to see me with their own goals and specific things they want to work on. If you're not good at speaking up in this way, no worries. Bring your notes and share them. Or make a short list of what you're having the most difficulty with. Or bring this book and point to the chapters you want help with. Your therapist can take it from there.

STRAIGHT TALK.

You'll notice that there are no statistics, summaries of research, or references to studies in this book. Nor do I use psychological jargon or talk about diagnoses, conditions, or kinds of therapy. It's not that these things aren't important. They are. But for our purposes, they're just going to get in the way. Or worse, they'll distract us from what's really needed, which is straight talk about you, your parents, and how you can get along better. That's it.

ABOVE ALL, BE KIND TO YOURSELF.

When you're done reading for the day—or even if you didn't read and are feeling bad about your relationships—please do something nice for yourself. I'm sure you've heard this before, but that's because it's important. Think about a simple thing you can do for yourself that feels comforting. Take a bath. Or a slow walk. Hang out with a pet. Watch a "guilty pleasure" TV show or movie that you've seen a dozen times. Whatever it is, try your best to enjoy it and remind yourself of these two things: You're doing good work, and you deserve to feel better.

FREQUENTLY ASKED QUESTIONS

Q: *Do my parents need to know I'm reading this book?*

A: No. You may choose to talk to them about the book, but it's not necessary. For now, it can be enough that you are reading, and taking steps to gain control and understanding of your life.

Q: *What if my parents have real (i.e., serious) problems? Am I supposed to become like a therapist and fix them?*

A: Absolutely not. You don't have to become your parents' therapist, nor do you have to take any responsibility for their problems. That's their job. What you will have to do is work on your relationship with your parents, but that's very different from trying to fix or "therapize" them.

Q: *Do I have to forgive them for things from the past? What if I'm not ready for that? What if I'm never going to be ready for that?*

A: It's okay. Strange as it seems, forgiveness isn't necessary to make your relationship better. Whether or not to forgive and how to do it are very personal decisions. It should always be up to you. Sometimes, well-intentioned people will tell you that you need to forgive in order to feel better and heal. This is a popular idea in our culture and it's easy to get pushed into believing it. But you can feel better about your relationships even if you're not ready to forgive.

Q: *What if my parents don't think they have any problems? What if they put it all on me, like I'm the one who's messed up?*

A: People—including parents—can think whatever they want. You might not be able to change that directly. But as you work through this book, *you* will begin to change. And when one person in a family changes, the others will change too. It's the physics of relationships, and it works regardless of whether a person knows about it.

Q: *What if other people—siblings, family friends, or even therapists—take my parents' side and see me as the problem? How am I supposed to change their minds?*

A: You're not. It might be hard to see it this way, but people can think whatever they want. We all can. It isn't your job to change their thoughts or feelings. We're going to concern ourselves here with *your* side of the story, not theirs. We're going to focus on your needs, not theirs.

Q: *I still don't understand why I have to read this book. My parents are the ones with the problems. Shouldn't* they *have to do the work? Shouldn't this responsibility fall on their shoulders and not mine?*

A: If you search online for books about parenting teens, you'll find a hundred or so great books. Did your parents read any of them? If so, did it make a difference? Maybe books aren't the right tool for them. But even if you could get your parents to read this particular book, it's not likely to make a difference because I didn't write it for them. It's for you, and it only works if *you* read it and do the work. That's not a guilt trip to get you to read. I know you'll do it if and when you're ready.

Q: What if I've only got a few months at home before I go off to college? My plan is to leave and never come back. I'm not going to talk to them after that.

A: Reading this book can make those last few months better. And even if you leave home and never talk to your parents again, understanding your connection to them will be important for the rest of your life. You will use what you learn to have better relationships with friends, partners, and even your partner's family.

STARTING WHERE WE ARE

Let's get right to it! There's a very specific reason you're reading this book, and that reason is that you're having problems with your parents. Or, more specifically, your parents have problems, and those problems are affecting you.

It might not be proper of me to say it so bluntly, but there it is. We must start where we are.

Here's where *I* am: After almost thirty years working with teens and their parents, I can tell you that the same scene keeps playing out. It's like *Groundhog Day*, but instead of Bill Murray and Andie MacDowell, it stars a bunch of teens and parents who are stuck in pain. Here's what that looks like: A pair of worried, stressed-out parents come into my office with their teen, a high school junior named Jay. The parents read off a laundry list of problems. There are bad grades, missing assignments, not enough sleep, panic attacks, and disordered eating. Meds haven't helped, and neither has therapy. The whole time Jay's parents are reading the list, Jay has their hood up and ear buds in. They're listening, though.

"We just want to find out what's wrong," says Jay's mom, "so we can get them the help they need."

"They used to be such a good student," Jay's dad adds. "They used to have friends and participate in band and sports."

This is where Jay completely tunes out. The floor tiles have suddenly become the most interesting thing in the room. Meanwhile, Dad says, "We'd like you to test for ADHD. Jay's brother has it and the meds have made a big difference. He's doing great, and we just want the same for Jay. We want Jay to get back on track with school and grades and be happy again."

Now check out what happens when the parents

leave. After a couple of questions, Jay looks up from the floor and clicks off their music. There's anger and hurt in their eyes.

"You know that was bullshit, right?" Jay says.

"Tell me," I say.

"My parents know exactly why I'm blowing off assignments and staying in my room all the time. They know exactly why I'm pissed off and unhappy."

I wait. Jay doesn't need me to pry it out of them. They have been thinking about this nonstop for months. They're ready to unload.

"First of all, they got divorced because my dad had an affair, and my mom is a total stress case because of her stupid super-important job. Now me and my little brother live between two apartments and have to deal with stepsiblings. And we're still expected to get perfect grades and do sports and clubs and activities and act like perfect, well-behaved offspring who don't complain and are grateful for everything. Last month I asked to drop AP Euro because I have no energy and can't keep up with the homework and exams. My mom said no because a withdrawal from an AP class will look 'suspicious' and hurt my chances of getting into a good college, which will make it harder for me to have a good career, buy a house, and raise my own family. And I'm thinking, 'Wait, you're both divorced, you hate your jobs, and none of us have talked with each other—like, really talked—in at least six months. So, I'm supposed to stay up till two a.m. doing homework so I can have the same kind of crappy life?' No thanks."

Let's take a moment to look at Jay's side of the story. It's different, for sure. I think it gives a much better explanation of why Jay's grades have slipped, and why Jay's been hiding in their room. But why didn't the parents share any of this information? Did they not notice? Did they deliberately hold back? There are lots of possible answers:

They genuinely—and incorrectly—believe that Jay's problems are a direct result of their poor choices. By the way, this is the explanation I hear most often, and here's why it's false: No one wakes up in the middle of a stable, satisfying life and says, "How boring! Now I think I'll try failing my classes, destroying my relationships, and becoming depressed. It's my life, and this is what I choose." Jay has reasons for their behavior. And those reasons are valid and important.

They consider family business to be private and don't want to put their dirty laundry out there for others to see. There has always been a strong taboo against talking about problems outside of the family, and this taboo usually causes harm. It further isolates teens at a time when they need support the most.

They feel guilty and embarrassed about their own choices, and are afraid of being judged as bad parents.

They have been so wrapped up in their own lives and problems that they haven't noticed.

They don't care about Jay's side of the story. Jay knows their expectations and needs to follow them. Period.

They are competitive with other parents, and don't want to reveal that they are falling short of their extremely high expectations.

They have bought into the myth of a perfect family and can't accept anything less.

Let's move on to the question of why Jay stayed quiet in my office while their parents were talking. It's clear that Jay's parents' life choices and behaviors have resulted in a lot of pain for Jay, and probably for Jay's little brother too. So why the silence? The possibilities here are more straightforward. These are the three I hear most often:

Staying quiet to avoid upsetting a delicate family balance.
"You don't know what it's like when I speak up. My dad starts yelling and then disappears to get drunk. My mom cries and says no one loves her. It's awkward for days, and I end up feeling like it's my fault. I should have just kept my mouth shut."

Avoiding adding more stress to parents who are already overwhelmed.

"My mom's dealing with a lot right now. She's raising us by herself and has her own problems. The last thing she needs is
me giving her more stress."

Thinking there's no point in speaking up. No one has ever listened before, so why bother?

"Trust me: They don't care. I've tried talking to them a million times. They don't listen. They hear only what they want to hear."

You might be thinking, "Okay, but why do I need to know all of this stuff about why parents act the way they do?" The reason is it's vital to know what's driving their behavior. What do they want from you? What are they afraid will happen if they don't act? Basically, you need to know about the attitudes and beliefs that make up their story of what's going on. In the example above, you can see that Jay's parents believe one story, while Jay believes another. What's needed is to merge these two versions into a single consistent story. When this is done, a new story is created. And, as far as stories go, it might not be uniformly happy—because life is rarely uniformly anything—but it will at least be true. True to both Jay and their parents.

THE NEW WORLD

There are three things you need to know about the world we're living in. First, it has changed. In a big way. I'm not just talking about things like politics and climate change. I'm talking about the actual landscape of adolescence. I'm talking about the places and spaces that people your age inhabit— to meet others, hang out, and build friendships and other relationships. These places and spaces are totally different from the ones your parents and older siblings knew about.

I'm sure you've seen it in old movies, how teens used to drive around together in cars, go to dances, and hang out at diners and burger joints. Some of that is pure nostalgia, sure, but there's truth in it too.

Teens did those things. They had whole lives that their parents didn't know about, or at least played no part in. Parents today are much more aware of the details of teens' lives through use of texting, tracking apps, and online networks. They keep track of events and performances, and may schedule things like tutoring, counseling, and college visits for their teens. People your age are much more likely to meet and hang out virtually now, and communicate through texting rather than voice, or social media rather than one-on-one communication. I'm not passing judgment about this, but I *am* saying that the shift from real to virtual has made it many times more difficult to get to know people, to hang out together, and to stay close.

Second, the effects of these changes are real and serious. Much of the sadness and loneliness that people have been feeling is a normal reaction to abnormal changes in the world. In addition to food, water, and clothing, human beings need frequent and direct social contact. Virtual is better than nothing, but it's not enough to meet the complex developmental needs of people your age. If that sounds too much like a textbook, I'm sorry, but it's important. In order to become an independent adult, you're going to need a lot of direct social contact with other people. In the last few years, the world hasn't been providing it.

Third, many parents aren't aware of just how much the world has changed. Or maybe they're aware of the changes, but not the degree to which the changes have affected their teens. Some parents are able to acknowledge the effects, but they don't accept that what they're seeing is a logical reaction to big changes in the world. They see it instead as a case of their teen making the wrong choices or not trying hard enough. Or losing their focus. Or picking the wrong friends. All incorrect.

What does this mean? It means that your parents aren't likely to understand how hard it is for you and your peers right now. They may not know that feeling lonely and isolated can be a normal reaction to abnormal world changes. Or that being distracted is a logical effect of living in a culture of technology. And they may see the struggle to find meaning in your life as boredom or apathy, which, of course, it's not.

I know this is sounding really negative, but there

are lots of reasons to be hopeful. For one, if you're unhappy with how things are going or with how you're feeling, you can learn to take control of your own life, starting with your relationships with your parents. You can learn to understand and accept your feelings and your true self. And then? You get the freedom to choose exactly how you want to live.

PARENT PROBLEMS: A CRASH COURSE

This is the part of the book where we talk about the very things we're not supposed to: your parents' problems. Why aren't we supposed to talk about them? Aside from the unspoken rules of our culture, parents are sensitive. They're also afraid. Afraid of doing a bad job and messing up their kids. Of repeating the mistakes their own parents made with them. Of being judged as bad parents. I know this because I'm a parent and I have the same fears. So do the thousands of parents I've talked to, whether or not they'll admit it publicly.

Here's the thing: It's culturally okay for parents

to talk openly about their teens' problems, but the opposite isn't true. Imagine two adults in a coffee shop. After a bit of small talk, one says, "How are your kids?" The other visibly winces. "John's good," he says, "but Claire is really struggling. She's been depressed and overwhelmed this semester. We just got her started on Prozac, and she's seeing a therapist. Hopefully she'll start to feel better and turn things around."

Can you imagine the same scene but with teens talking about their parents? I know: Self-respecting teens would never ask each other about their parents. But imagine if they did. One boy saying, "What's up, Jules? How's it going with you and your parents?" And Jules answering, "I'm fine, but my dad drinks too much and has totally checked out from the family. My mom is a workaholic and a control freak, and she takes it out on me by monitoring my grades and scheduling college tours instead of family vacations. How are you and your parents?"

Ridiculous, I know. The goal here isn't to level the playing field of complaints or disclosures. The goal is to be honest about the kinds of parent problems that teens like you are dealing with. To be honest, we have to name these problems and describe them. We need to talk about the effects these problems have had on you.

We also need to uncover the reasons parents might have these problems. This is not to forgive them or let them off the hook. It's about understanding the *why* behind problematic behaviors. Put another way, we're talking about the reasons parents act in ways that disrupt relationships. Please believe me when I say this isn't a ploy to garner sympathy for your parents. The goal of this section is to increase understanding, which is crucial for the work that lies ahead. The thing about understanding is it gives you a little distance from your emotions. This is especially important if your emotions are intense and powerful. The extra distance allows you to feel the emotions without the need to act on them. This is necessary for change.

Still skeptical? That's okay. Just know that if your parents are acting in harmful ways and you want to change their behavior, you first need to figure out what's driving it. It's a matter of asking: "What do they want from their relationship with me? What are they trying to get: validation, friendship, respect from their friends, or peace and quiet? A boost in their own self-esteem? Success through me?" This is really important. Remember, we're not trying to therapize or fix your parents. We're trying to understand what motivates them so you can use that information to manage difficult situations better.

What follows are descriptions of problem behaviors that many parents engage in. They're grouped in categories, not diagnoses or labels. They're written in the plural *parents* for convenience. A description may only apply to one of your parents. It's also possible for several descriptions to apply to one parent. Yet another possibility is for one of these descriptions to apply perfectly, but only at certain times, like when there's a lot of stress at home or at your parent's job.

The point of this section is for you to see the behaviors that certain *types of parents* engage in, and to learn a little about why they might be doing this. The goal is to take a part of your life that might be vague and confusing (your dad yelled at you, but maybe he didn't mean it, and maybe you're being too sensitive) and move it to a space that is real and concrete (your dad yelled and you feel hurt, and that's not okay).

You might want to skip the categories and simply say that all these parents act badly because they are emotionally immature; they don't have the skills needed for emotional connection. In many cases this is true, and it's a useful way of looking at the problem. But I'm afraid that doing so might skip the important step of naming and describing exactly what you've been dealing with at home. Because it's real, we need to treat it that way by naming and describing it.

Lastly, the descriptions below make up only a partial list. I've left off some of the more obvious ones that are commonly understood and talked about. For example, *self-destructive parents* may abuse drugs and alcohol, take unnecessary risks, or hurt themselves in various other ways. *Passive-aggressive parents* tell their teens that things are okay while acting out their anger or dissatisfaction in subtle but obvious ways. *Parents with a special needs family member* may become so consumed with that person's care that they have little time or energy for you.

COMPLAINING AND CRITICIZING

Description

These parents find fault with people, things, or maybe just with you. They might complain about the service at a restaurant, the way you set the table, or the kind of friends you hang out with. They complain often and at length and can't seem to let it go and move on, even when asked to do so. They rarely have a positive thing to say about others and can go on at length about people's shortcomings and faults.

Effects

Teens living with parents who complain and criticize often respond in two ways. The first is to try to make the parents happy, in hopes that they will become more pleasant or find someone else to complain about. As you might guess, this rarely works because a) it's impossible to change another person's mood and outlook, and b) the complaining isn't really about you, even if it seems that way. It's instead a negative way of relating to the world. This may be hard to believe, but complaining and criticizing actually have little to do with you, though it may seem very personal.

The second way of responding is avoidance. If you're living under the cloud of constant complaints and criticism, you may hide in your room, stay out with friends, and avoid unnecessary interaction or conversation with your parents. This may reduce conflict, but it also increases distance and leads to anger, resentment, and a feeling that you don't belong.

Reasons why

Parents who complain and criticize excessively are often very dissatisfied with their lives and don't feel that they have a lot of control. They may feel disrespected or unappreciated. Or they feel as if they work too hard for too little reward. Some will cite hurts or wounds from the past as justifications, while others may have very little insight at all, believing that the world around them is filled with incompetent, annoying, and ungrateful people.

Response style

It's not common for these parents to be called out on their behavior. The reason is that they're unpleasant to deal with. It's much easier to avoid them. If they are challenged, however, they're likely to respond with even more complaints or outright anger. A typical response would be to double down on the complaint or criticism.

A typical conversation

Julia: Mom, I've got good news. I got an A on my geometry test. I was really worried about it, but the teacher said I got the second-highest score in the class.

Mom: Mr. Bradley? God, he taught when I was a student there. He was a terrible teacher. I didn't learn a thing. Do you know how much that man makes? And it comes from *my* taxes.

Julia: I'm thinking of taking advanced algebra next year. I really like math.

Mom: Why? Do you want to be a math teacher, like Mr. Bradley?

Julia: No. But—

Mom: Then why bother studying something that a calculator can do in two seconds? I don't understand why schools keep pushing these old career paths that aren't even relevant anymore.

Julia: Mom, I'm just saying—

Mom: Advanced math, I know. But what do you think is going to happen in the middle of the semester when it gets too hard for you? I'm not paying for a tutor again. Been there, done that.

ARGUING

Description

These parents start arguments and respond to others' comments or conversations in an argumentative way. They blame others and stick rigidly to their own beliefs and ideas, even when the topic at hand is meaningless or irrelevant. It's almost as if they have a need to pick fights or contradict others. Some parents argue mainly with each other, some argue with just you or your siblings, and still others argue with everyone. Some parents are careful about their arguing and only do it at home, while others eagerly let it rip in public.

Effects

If you live with parents who argue you might feel as if you're walking on eggshells when you're around them because you never know when the next argument is going to arrive. And so, the only thing to do is brace for it. Or retreat. You might feel nervous or tense. It might be difficult to relax and let your guard down. Or to get to sleep at night, especially if the day's arguments are replaying in your head. Similarly, it might be hard to shift into other activities like studying or hanging out with friends, especially if the effects of a recent argument are still lingering.

Reasons why

Many parents who argue justify the behavior by saying things like "That's how I grew up. We were a big loud family" and "Everybody yelled at each other all the time. It didn't mean anything. It's just how we related." Some parents argue because they can't tolerate the idea of being wrong, or because they immaturely believe that the world and other people are supposed to be a certain way. When reality doesn't conform, it's upsetting, and they feel compelled to argue about it.

Response style

Denial is a common response from parents who argue. If you ask why they're arguing with you—perhaps about something that doesn't even concern them, or something they don't even care about—they're likely to say, "I'm not arguing. I'm just sharing my opinion. Am I not allowed to have an opinion in my own house?"

A typical conversation

Dad: I heard Wegman's is hiring. Did you apply?

Juan: No. Wegman's is always hiring, and I want to work at the coffee shop. I already interviewed, and they said they were going to call this week.

Dad: So you can't apply anywhere else? What if the coffee shop doesn't call? What then?

Juan: Then I'll apply at Wegman's. But I think I'm going to get this job, Dad. It pays tips too.

Dad: So what you're saying is you're too good to work at Wegman's?

Juan: I didn't say that at all. I said I'd work at Wegman's if the other job falls through.

Dad: I see. You'd rather make seven-dollar lattes for rich jerks than do honest work. Is that it?

OVERINVOLVED

Description

These parents are extremely focused on their teen in a way that is controlling and overprotective. They may micromanage every aspect of their teen's life. They often worry excessively and try to manage how others treat their teen. They will go to great lengths to make sure that their teen doesn't experience discomfort, failure, or emotional pain. Examples include doing their teen's homework for them; bullying teachers into boosting grades and providing unnecessary accommodations; pushing coaches to give more playing time; and even problem-solving with their teen's friends after disagreements.

Effects

Overinvolved parenting denies teens the opportunity to make independent decisions and learn from their mistakes. Teens with overinvolved parents often suffer from low self-confidence, anxiety, a sense of entitlement, and poor coping skills. Perhaps the worst effect is that of the teen feeling incompetent, since many of the overinvolved parenting behaviors give this message: "I have to do all of these things for you because I really don't think you can do them successfully on your own."

Reasons why

On the surface, many overinvolved parents act out of worry, but the worry comes from difficulty managing their own anxiety. Peer pressure from other overinvolved parents often makes the situation worse, exaggerating existing tendencies. Some overinvolved parents are trying to deal with feelings of emptiness or lack of fulfillment. Still others are driven by their own perfectionism, which they act out through their parenting. Overinvolved parents are often goal-obsessed, rigid, super busy, always trying to perfect everything—including other people. They're likely to see their children as reflections of themselves.

Response style

When challenged, overinvolved parents respond by stating—and restating—their commitment to your wellbeing or success. "I'm only doing this for your own good." Sometimes they'll bring up the subject of goals, but are oblivious to the fact that it's their goals thinly veiled as yours. "I'm doing this because you want to get into Princeton, and this is what it takes."

A typical conversation

Mom: Did you check your Canvas account? I saw that your econ assignment wasn't turned in yesterday. What were you thinking?

Simona: It's okay. I'll finish it in study hall today and turn it in sixth period.

Mom: Doesn't your teacher deduct points for being late?

Simona: Yes, but just five. I'll get, like, a ninety-five.

Mom: That's not okay. You shouldn't have any points deducted.

Simona: Mom.

Mom: I'll email the teacher and let him know you've had three other exams this week, plus hockey playoffs. And if he still gives you a hard time, I can have the 504 Coordinator add extra time on assignments to your plan. Then the teacher will have no choice.

Simona: Mom, really, it's okay—

Mom: It's not, kiddo. You have to keep your weighted GPA up if there's any chance of getting into your top schools. Oh, and don't forget: You're meeting with the French tutor after school.

UNINVOLVED

Description

Uninvolved parents provide little support for their teens and make few if any demands. They rarely set or enforce rules, nor do they offer guidance, support, or give expectations. They may skip school events and pay little attention to what's going on in their teen's life. They show little warmth or affection.

Effects

Uninvolved parenting makes it difficult for you to assess expectations and limits in different situations. You may have a harder time forming relationships, because the rules of relationships at home aren't clear—or may be totally missing. You may struggle with social skills and may have to learn them on your own. An especially confusing variation is when uninvolved parents get divorced and show energy and interest in their new partners and/or stepchildren. This may lead you to question your own value and wonder, "Wait, what's so different or special about them?"

Reasons why

Uninvolved parents are often busy or preoccupied with their own lives and problems. They may be fixated on work, hobbies, or other pursuits. Their attention may be consumed by their own health problems or those of other family members. Some may be in the midst of drug and/or alcohol abuse. Others may have been raised by uninvolved parents and see it as normal.

Response style

When challenged on their behavior, uninvolved parents respond in one of two ways. First, they may lie or deny. "That's not true. I might have been five minutes late, but I've never been two hours late." The second way is to reframe the scope of their responsibility. They may put it back on you: "I work and put food on the table. What more do you want from me? I'm supposed to . . . what, follow you around and ask how you're feeling?"

A typical conversation

Keisha: I looked for you in the stands.

Dad: Yeah, I had some stuff to do.

Keisha: It was the last game of the season.

Dad: What do you want from me? I was busy.

Keisha: I just thought it would be nice if you came to one game in my senior year. You know, before I go off to college.

Dad: Look. I pay for food and clothes and ski club and whatever else you need. Isn't that enough?

Keisha: I appreciate those things. I do. But—

Dad: Then don't guilt-trip me. My parents weren't involved in my life and it didn't mean they didn't love me. They were too busy working and paying the bills. That's exactly what I'm doing.

DISTRACTED

Description

This one most commonly applies to parents who are constantly on their phones, checking messages and emails, posting on social media, or otherwise distracting themselves from whatever is happening in the moment. It could just as easily apply to other activities, like TV watching, reading, tinkering, or even belonging to a club or group. The distracted parent will often be around you, but they're not looking, listening, or engaging. They respond to your questions or requests with "Wait a second," and interrupt conversations suddenly to check their phones or busy themselves with something else.

Effects

Teens of distracted parents often wonder whether they matter. They may doubt that they have anything of interest or value to share. Or they may become equally distracted.

Reasons why

Distracted parents are often bored or unfulfilled. They may also be self-absorbed, especially if they're spending excessive time on social media, posting and keeping up with others' posts. They may be workaholics. Whatever the reason, they're likely unaware of how distracted and disconnected they are. They may even feel that their behavior is justified, especially if they're distracted by work or something they feel is important.

Response style

Distracted parents typically deny that they're distracted. "I'm here. See?" Or "I'm paying attention now. What do you want?"

A typical conversation

Malik: Mom, did you hear me?

Mom: What?

Malik: I asked if we're having dinner tonight of if I should get something myself?

Mom: Hold on a second. Brenda from work is texting me something.
Malik: *sigh*

Mom (putting phone down): You know, not everything is about you, Malik.

Malik: I know, Mom. I was just asking—

Mom (picking phone up again): What do you want? Just say it. I don't have all day.

ALOOF OR EMOTIONALLY UNAVAILABLE

Description

Aloof parents are not distracted; they are emotionally unavailable. They provide for basic needs and may even participate in activities and other parts of family life, but they are almost always distant, appearing cut off or as if they're somewhere else. They tend to avoid physical contact and may not give hugs or say "I love you." They tend to have few close friendships and are generally uncomfortable around displays of emotion or affection.

Effects

It's easy to feel unloved by an aloof parent. Some teens become excessively cheerful or helpful in an attempt to try to squeeze a little affection from the parent, or to prove their worth. Others give up trying and withdraw. Still others find solace in friends and in the families of friends, especially those who are warm and accepting.

Reasons why

Many of these parents were raised by aloof parents and didn't get enough love and attention when they were children. This isn't always the case, however. Some grew up in warm and loving homes but were reserved and distant as children. Some are extremely analytical and prefer to relate to others through work or shared interests. Many aloof parents explain their behavior by saying things like, "This is how I am" and "I don't see the need in saying I love you all the time or giving hugs. It doesn't feel right for me."

Response style

It's unusual for an aloof parent to be challenged about their behavior. The main reason for this is that it's so hard to put your finger on what, exactly, the behavior is or looks like. After all, it's an absence of behavior. No connection. No awareness of your emotions. But when questioned, they may have a hard time even understanding the complaint. "I don't understand what you want from me."

A typical conversation

Lydia: Guess what, Dad? I got the part in the school play.

Dad: That's great. Good job.

Lydia: Do you want to hear about it? The auditions were super long and intense.

Dad: Maybe later.

Lydia: Well, I'm really excited. I didn't think I'd get the part, but Mrs. Jordan said I totally nailed it. What if we get some ice cream to celebrate? I checked and they're still open.

Dad: I've got a project I'm working on in the garage, but good job with the play.

Lydia: Are you even proud of me?

Dad: Of course. What do you want from me here? I said good job.

UNPREDICTABLE

Description

Unpredictable parents can become hostile, angry, dramatic, or cruel, often with little reason. They may act inconsistently from one situation to another. Some yell, slam doors, or throw things. Others swing from happy and easygoing to upset, sometimes without apparent cause. The unpredictable behavior may appear during a specific situation—like in the case of road rage—or episodically, every few days or even every few weeks.

Effects

Teens living with unpredictable parents often feel a great deal of anxiety and fear. A sense of low self-worth may result, and teens may hide or find reasons to be out of the house or away from their parents. Some teens will seek out friendships or partners that appear to offer stability and predictability.

Others may become overachievers, joining every club or activity. They may think that, if they become the perfect teen, it will make up for the chaos at home, or at least it won't be visible to others.

Reasons why

Unpredictable parents often experienced childhood chaos and abuse. Substance use/abuse is a common contributor, as is feeling generally out of control. These parents often explain their behavior by making comparisons to their own childhood to highlight how much worse they had it. "You want to see chaos? Try coming home to a drunk father who likes to hit. I might lose my temper sometimes, but I never hit any of my kids. I'd never do that to them." In general, though, unpredictable parents haven't learned to regulate their own emotions. Many have shockingly poor impulse control. They often have low tolerance for frustration too. All of this means that they don't have the emotional equipment needed to handle close relationships or the demands ofparenting.

Response style

Unpredictable parents respond . . . unpredictably.

They may argue, cry, make fun of you, or leave. They may stomp around the house, slamming doors and cupboards, or they may quietly get drunk or high. Whatever form the behavior takes, however, it all stems from the same thing: They aren't able to control their emotions. Being challenged about their behavior is extremely threatening to them; they don't have the skills to respond in any other way.

A typical conversation

Elleanor: Is Dad home?

Jack: Can't you tell? It's quiet.

Elleanor (whispering, even though their father isn't at home): He got really mad this morning. He was dropping me off at school and some guy cut in front of him at the parking lot.

Jack: Jesus. I'm glad I wasn't there to see that. Did Principal Murphy have to get involved?

Elleanor: No, but it was so embarrassing, Jack. He

got out of the car and banged on the guy's window, and do you know who it was?

Jack: Who?

Elleanor: Dashawn Miller's grandfather.

Jack (cradling his head in his hands): I don't want to hear any more.

YOUR EMOTIONAL BLUEPRINT

It's likely that none of the examples above fully describes your parents. Many teens I talk to explain that theirs have characteristics of several of the parent types. They might be primarily aloof and distracted, but at times they can be volatile and unpredictable. Or maybe they act in ways I haven't touched on yet.

Now we're going to shift from your parents' problem behaviors to your feelings. Specifically, when they act in careless or hurtful ways, what does it feel like to you?

Think of the checklist below as a blueprint for your emotional experience growing up in your family. Put an X next to the statements that describe how you feel. Later, we'll use those items to build a plan for how to talk to your parents differently, and how to set and hold boundaries around their problem behaviors.

If you find that you're having trouble deciding which apply to you, don't overthink it. This isn't a scientific instrument. And we're not using it to come up with a diagnosis. What's your gut feeling? Take your best guess. Later, when we're working on scripts for conversations and boundaries, you can look back at the items you checked to help focus the script on what's most important.

If you're still nervous about any item on this checklist, ask yourself, "Have I felt this way in the past month?" If so, put an X in the blank space. If you've only felt this way once or twice in your whole life but not in a while, leave it blank.

Lastly, this is a very long list but it's not exhaustive.If you don't find some of your parents' problem behaviors, write them in on the blank spaces at the bottom. And consider emailing me so I can include them in future editions.

_____ I feel invisible or unseen by my parents.

_____ I don't feel heard or listened to by my parents.

_____ I don't feel like my parents understand me or get me.

_____ I feel like my parents' mood is contagious; they want me to feel upset if they're upset, happy when they're happy, and sad when they're sad.

_____ I feel empty and alone when I'm around my parents.

_____ I've had to learn to ignore my own feelings.

_____ I feel guilty for being in a good mood because my parents aren't ever happy.

_____ I'm afraid of saying how I really feel because my parents might say I'm too sensitive or dramatic.

_____ My parents' needs always come first.

_____ I feel like I've had to grow up too fast and missed out on being a kid.

_____ I feel like I've had to learn to get by with little to no emotional support.

_____ I've fantasized about being better/smarter/more popular/more successful so that my parents will have to love me.

_____ I worry that if I'm honest about my feelings and my needs, my parents will cut me off or shut me out.

_____ I feel like it's my job to please my parents and make them feel better.

_____ I've dreamed of getting a real apology from my parents, but I know it will never happen.

_____ When I spend a lot of time with my parents, I end up feeling guilty, bad, or ashamed, even though I haven't done anything wrong.

_____ When I spend a lot of time with my parents, I feel tired, exhausted, or emotionally drained.

_____ I feel as if I do all the work to maintain a connection with my parents. If I stop, there won't be any connection at all.

_____ Whenever I try to talk to my parents it ends in an argument.

_____ I agree to things I don't want just to avoid conflict.

_____ I agree to things I don't want just to avoid a guilt trip from my parents.

_____ I feel nervous, frightened, or uncomfortable around my parents.

_____ I feel as if the bad things that happened to me are my own fault.

_____ I feel unlikeable or unlovable.

_____ I feel used and unappreciated.

_____ I feel as if I've missed out on having a real childhood or adolescence.

_____ I don't feel like I can trust my parents.

_____ I feel like I'm unable to experience joy.

_____ I feel like I've lost my innocence.

_____ I feel anxious and overwhelmed when I spend time with my parents.

_____ I feel sad and lonely around my parents.

_____ I feel depressed and hopeless around my parents.

_____ I feel confused and unsure of myself around my parents.

_____ I feel criticized or judged by my parents.

_____ I feel as if my parents have trapped me into taking care of them.

_____ I feel like my confidence is gone and I can no longer trust my instincts.

_____ I feel like my relationship with my parents is one-sided.

_____ I feel like whatever I get from my parents comes with too many strings. Most of the time it's not worth it.

_____ When I'm around my parents I have to pretend to be cheerful and happy when I'm not.

_____ I hide my emotions from my parents so I won't upset them.

_____ I can't say no to my parents. They get too upset.

_____ I can't stand up to my parents.

_____ I get anxious or scared at the thought of confronting my parents.

_____ I avoid my parents by staying in my room, being out with friends, or staying late at school.

_____ I worry about certain topics coming up because it will cause an argument or an unwanted lecture.

_____ In my free time and at night I find myself going over old arguments or conversations, thinking about what I should have said.

_____ I don't feel like I can have my own beliefs and values. My parents expect me to think and believe exactly what they do.

_____ My parents don't respect my time or privacy.

_____ I look forward to the times when my parents are out of the house.

_____ I feel ashamed when my parents trash-talk my friends or other family members.

_____ I feel disrespected when my parents don't recognize names, pronouns, or gender identities.

_____ I feel like I'm worthy only when I run
      my parents' errands, cook, babysit, etc.

_____

_____

_____

_____

_____

_____

_____

_____

_____

_____

_____

_____

Go back and take a look at your responses. I'm
not going to ask you to do anything with them other
than acknowledge them. These feelings are part of
your emotional experience growing up with parents
who have problems forming close relationships.

These feelings are not right or wrong, but they are 100 percent valid. And they have absolutely nothing to do with who you are as a person. Neither do they predict the kind of life you will have in the future. Think of it more as a snapshot of where you're at right now. A starting point.

It's not unusual to have new emotions come to the surface after doing this exercise. You might be sad or angry upon seeing the items you checked. This is okay. Do your best to sit with the emotions for a little while. Remind yourself that these emotions are real and valid, and you don't have to explain or make sense of them. If, after twenty or thirty minutes, the feelings haven't lessened in intensity, put the book down and take a break. You've done difficult and important work, and you deserve to do something nice for yourself.

REPAIRING DISCONNECTION

The parents I've been describing so far couldn't be more different, but they have one thing in common: disconnection. It's at the heart of most parent-teen conflicts. Even overinvolved parents are disconnected. They mistake spending lots of time with their teens for real connection, which is the product of understanding and acceptance, not micromanaging and controlling others.

At the opposite end of the spectrum is the uninvolved parent who doesn't seem to notice or care. The lack of connection here is obvious, but the effects on their teen are the same: loneliness, frustration, and resentment.

As complicated as these problems may seem, the fix is obvious: to increase connection.

One way to do this is to talk to your parents. You might be thinking, "Yeah, right. I've tried, but they don't listen." Or "No way. I can't talk to my mom. We don't see eye to eye." Or "Every time I try and talk to my dad it blows up into a big argument, and then it's awkward for days. The rest of the family ends up having to tiptoe around him, and they blame me." If you've had these kinds of experiences, don't worry: There are many ways to make it easier. You're even going to learn several skills that don't require talking at all.

SETTING ASIDE HURTS AND PAST ARGUMENTS— FOR JUST TWO MINUTES!

The goal here is to start very small. I'm talking two minutes or less. In that span of time, you're going to try to accomplish two things. First, you're going to be in the same room or space with your parents. If you've been avoiding each other, this may be difficult. Acknowledge the difficulty and try it anyway. The reason here is simple: If you're going to improve your relationship with your parents, you all have to learn—or relearn—how to be in the same space together.

The second part: During those two minutes, try setting aside the anger, hurt, or resentment you've been feeling toward your parents. Notice I said *setting aside*. That's not the same thing as ignoring your parents' bad behavior or the way it makes you feel. Or the past. You're not going to forget about it. You're not going to forgive them. What you will do is set those feelings aside for two minutes or less and then, when you're done, pick them back up again. That's right. As soon as the two minutes are up, you can go back to being angry, hurt, or resentful. You haven't let your parents off the hook for anything. Neither have you compromised your integrity or values; you're still the same person you were two minutes ago.

You might be thinking, "Fine, but how do I *set aside* my emotions? That doesn't sound very realistic. Or therapeutic." The reality is that our emotions change all the time. We shift in and out of them. When we focus on them, they intensify. And when we shift our focus away from them, they lessen.

The problem is, when we repeatedly experience intense and negative emotions about another person, we learn to associate those feelings with them. To put it another way, just seeing that person—or hearing their voice, or their approaching footsteps—can stir up those feelings. This practice is going to interrupt, for just two minutes, the connection between your parents and the negative emotions you've felt in their presence.

A common question is, "What do I do in those two minutes?" Anything you want. You don't have to talk, but if you do, keep it light. Ask about their day. Share something about your day that isn't likely to invite a lot of questions or unwanted lectures. If you don't want to talk, busy yourself with something. Pretend to read a book, or get yourself something to drink and sit until you finish it.

Troubleshooting

If you're thinking, "Forget it. I'm not going to be fake. If I'm mad, I'm mad," that's valid too. But you're not going to compromise your integrity or values by talking to someone for two minutes. You've probably done this plenty of times with friends, teachers, or a rude cashier. Chances are you were mad but still able to complete the transaction.

Maybe your parents will notice your presence and respond with a sarcastic comment. Something like, "To what do we owe this pleasure?" Or "So you've finally decided to come out of your room and join the real world?" It's likely to bring up a lot of feelings very quickly, but try to take this as a sign of change. You've changed your behavior and they noticed! You don't have to respond at all, but if you do, keep it short and mild. "Yes," works surprisingly well, as does, "Just taking a break." I'm not a fan of sarcasm, but if you can pull it off, humor works great. "Don't worry: I'll return to the darkness and solitude of my room in a couple of minutes."

If this strategy doesn't sit right with you, or feels like too much too soon, respect your instincts. Move on.

GOOD DISTRACTIONS

Good distractions are the perfect place to start because they don't require a lot of energy or effort, and they minimize conversation. If that seems counterproductive—since the very goal of this chapter is to talk more—think of it as setting the stage for future conversations. You've heard the saying "Before you can run, you need to learn to walk"? Well, in this case, before you and your parents can get into some real and difficult conversations, you need to learn to tolerate being around each other for short periods of time.

If you're scowling right now, thinking, "No thanks. I want to spend as little time as possible around my mom," or "I wouldn't even know how to ask my dad to do something together. It would sound stupid, and he'd probably say no," here are some easy ways to ask:

Remember when we used to go to the diner for breakfast (or whatever activity the two of you used to do)? Want to go?

Come for a walk with me. Just a short one.

Will you take me for a driving lesson? I need practice.

How about we watch TV tonight? I'll make popcorn.

Let's go to the dog park (or the coffee shop/gym/store).

Want some help cooking dinner (or washing the car, or whatever they might be doing)?

The best distractions are activities that are fairly complete in and of themselves. TV and listening to music are especially good because it's hard to talk while watching or listening. This takes away some of the burden of conversation. Bonus points if you can find a show or music that you both like. And if you happen to find a show with multiple seasons, that can become a shared activity that can last weeks or even longer. It can give the two of you something to look forward to, and maybe even something to talk about later.

The reason distractions work is twofold. First, a good distraction is a low-pressure way to connect. Second, it provides a short, limited block of time in which your parent can learn a little about you. Shouldn't they already know? Yes, but if there has been a lot of conflict, it's likely that you and your parents have been actively avoiding each other.

For months or even years. It's also likely that your parents did a better job connecting with you and meeting your needs when you were little. They may not have made the shift as you grew older and your needs and interests changed.

Troubleshooting

If you tried and it went horribly wrong—couldn't decide on which show to watch and started arguing, for example—don't sweat it. Back off for a day or two and try it again, but with a different activity. Or take the pressure off by placing the time of the activity in the future. Ask your parents to pick some movies they might want to watch in the future. Or a recipe you might cook together at a later date. It's easier to go along with something new and potentially uncomfortable when it's a week or two away. Then, when you refer back to it, they've already agreed.

Maybe the situation between you and your parents is too sensitive. In this case, you may not be ready to spend time with them. It's okay. Trust your instincts and allow for the possibility of feeling differently in the future.

RIGHT TIME/WRONG TIME

Picking the right time to talk to your parent can make a huge difference. The wrong time can doom the conversation from the start. If this seems obvious, it is, but it's also hugely neglected as a strategy. It's a fact that our lives today are busier than ever, and finding time when both you and your parents are relaxed and open can seem almost impossible. But even in the busiest families there are times of the day that are decidedly better or worse. Consider this scenario:

Joan, a fifty-two-year-old single mother, finishes work an hour late after receiving a less-than-stellar evaluation from her supervisor. Typically, her commute home takes twenty minutes. Today, however, she has to pick up a prescription at the pharmacy, drop off her dry-cleaning, and grab a pizza for dinner. By the time she arrives home, the pizza is cold and she realizes it's the wrong one—pepperoni and sausage instead of vegan. Worse, she's feeling the beginnings of a headache. But when she gets in the door she sees that her daughter, Claire, has been waiting for her, eager to talk about something that happened at school.

Claire: Good, you're home. We need to talk!

Joan (setting her bags down and pinching the bridge of her nose): Give me a minute to get settled?

Claire (after waiting): Okay, you're not going to believe what happened earlier. Do you remember that situation I was telling you about with William and Tatiana?

Joan (looking on the verge of tears): Claire, this actually isn't a good time.

Claire (sighing, looking hurt and on the verge of tears herself): Fine. I guess I just won't tell you about my life anymore.

Let's play out the same conversation, but it's two hours later. Joan has just taken a bath. She is relaxing on the couch with the family cat purring contentedly on her lap.

Claire: Mom, do you want to hear a crazy story that happened at school today?

Joan: Definitely.

Claire: Remember my friends William and Tatiana?

Joan (thinking, remembering): You went to middle school together?

Claire: Right, but they've been dating for all of this past year. You're not going to believe what just happened.

Joan: Tell me about it.

Totally different, right? But you might be thinking, "Wait, my parents are irritable and distracted *all* the time." Try observing them for a few days. Maybe they're more open to talking early in the morning.

Maybe they're especially miserable when they haven't eaten. Or angry and stressed right after work. Or relaxed while walking the dog. Do some detective work and learn their patterns. Then time your conversations accordingly.

Troubleshooting

Maybe your parents are too unpredictable. You've observed their habits and schedules and there truly are no patterns. Take a shot and ask: "Want to watch a show?" Sometimes, if you and your parents haven't connected in a very long time, they might be too surprised to say no. "What, you mean like right now? With me?" "Yes. Now. With *me*."

Maybe your parents are too irritable/distracted/ unavailable. In this case, put it to them as a question: "I'd like to talk/hang out/do something together, but I know you're busy. Can you let me know in the next week if you have the time and energy?" If a few days go by and they don't say anything, give a reminder. "Remember when I asked you about doing something together? Well, how about now?" If the answer is no, say, "No problem. Another time?"

CATCHING GOOD

This one is straight-up manipulative, so pay attention! I should add that it's also really powerful, and you might find yourself using it with siblings, friends, and even your teachers.

Catching Good is based on the principle that even a broken clock is accurate twice a day. What this means is that the most distracted parent will pay attention once in a while, and a critical parent will slip up occasionally and say something nice—or at least *not mean*. Even a terminally unreliable parent will arrive on time once or twice.

Your job is to catch the rare example of good parenting and make it stick, which is to say make it happen more often. How do you do that? There are three simple steps:

Notice. Be on the lookout for the behavior you'd like to see more of. It could be a rare compliment, a moment of compassion, or an acknowledgment of your hard-earned grade in a class. Maybe it's that your busy, preoccupied father remembers to pick up your favorite ice cream when he's at the grocery store. Whatever the behavior, note it when it occurs.

An interesting side effect is that once you start looking for something—whether it's a purple car or the odd example of good behavior from your parents—you see it more often. I know I promised not to use jargon or technical talk, but this one is too good not to share. It's called the frequency bias, or the Baader-Meinhof phenomenon. Throw that around the next time you're hanging out with your friends! Actually, don't. You'll get strange looks.

Resist the urge to explain it away. Instead of saying "She's only being nice because she wants something from me," or "This doesn't make up for all the times he was rude and called me names," try to accept the compliment. It might not happen very often, but that doesn't mean it's not valid.

Most important, point it out to your parents. Draw their attention to the behavior and let them know that you like it and wouldn't mind if it happened again. You don't have to have a big discussion about it. Just be clear and specific. Here are a few examples:

"It makes me feel good when you tell me I'm a good student."

"Thanks for sitting down and talking. It means a lot."

"That was fun watching a movie together. Let's do it again."

"I like shopping together."

"Thanks for bringing me takeout. It was really good and I appreciate it."

You'd be surprised how effective this one can be. Many parents want to help their teens be happy but have no idea how. This gives them specific information on how to do it. And for parents who are under the weird assumption that they're supposed to have deep serious talks (that they couldn't possibly pull off anyway), you're letting them off the hook. You're saying, "If you want to spend time with me and connect, there are lots of easy ways to do this and I'll give you some examples."

Troubleshooting

What if you observe your parents carefully, but there's nothing good to work with? In this case, consider complimenting them on some ordinary thing, like,

"Thanks for picking me up from work the other day."
If your parent responds by saying, "I pick you up every
Wednesday," say, "Yeah, and I appreciate it." They
might be totally confused, but that's okay. Showing
appreciation works even if it's made up!

Maybe you catch your parents doing something
good such as complimenting you on your latest
English essay, but they follow it up with a criticism.
"You did an amazing job in English, but we're definitely not happy with that grade in math. You can do
way better, and don't expect to be going . . ."

In this case, don't bother trying to deal with the
criticism part of the statement. Focus on the first
part. Say, "Thanks for noticing and commenting on
the English essay. I worked hard on it and it means
a lot." If your parents are especially persistent about
the criticism part, try being persistent yourself.
Double down on the compliment part: ". . . and I still
appreciate you noticing and commenting on my
English essay."

BUYING TIME

Sometimes it's just not possible to do heavy emotional

work. Maybe you're going through something with a friend or boyfriend or girlfriend. Maybe you're in the middle of exams, or you're working long hours to save up for a car. Whatever the circumstances, if you're feeling especially drained but still want to do the work outlined in this book, consider buying yourself some time.

What this means is deciding on a specific interval, whether it's a week, a month, or longer, and during this time, not engaging in actively trying to repair or improve your relationship with your parents. You will not spend time rehashing old arguments or worrying about what your parents will say in future conversations.

You might be thinking, "Cool, but how is this different from doing nothing?" When you do nothing, you're not making any changes at all. When you *buy time*, however, you're making a single big change: You're shifting from "I can't" to "I can't *right now*." And from "I'm not ready" to "I'm not ready yet, *but I will be*."

This might not sound like a big difference, but it is. You're not letting yourself off the hook from doing important work; you're giving yourself the precious gift of more time, and that will likely increase the effectiveness of that work when you're ready to do it. This is an act of compassion. It's such a big deal because we're often harder on ourselves then we are on others. Way harder. Giving yourself time is one way to show kindness. Here are the steps:

1) Be clear about what's getting in the way of you doing this work now. Name it specifically. An example is, "I can't do this work yet because I'm in the middle of a breakup with my boyfriend."

2) Decide on the amount of time you need. Be generous but not excessive. "I need three weeks to get through the end of play rehearsals. After that, in early May, I'll get back to it. Again, write it down to hold yourself accountable.

3) Protect your time and mental space when situations interfere. Things will continue to happen, but when you find yourself angry, sad, and confused, say, "Okay, I knew this would happen, but I've got another couple of weeks. I

don't have to do anything about this now. I especially don't have to stress or worry about it."

Troubleshooting

Say you give yourself a couple of weeks but at the end you still don't feel ready. In this case, give yourself more time. It's okay. It's even okay if you need to put this book back on the shelf for a month or two or even longer. Come back to it when you're ready.

What if you try to buy yourself time but feel like you can't ignore your parent problems? Maybe there has been a crisis. Or the conflict between you and your parents is too much to tolerate, even though you want to focus on other things. In this case, it's likely a situation in which you need to set a boundary. Go to the chapter that begins on page 137, which is all about boundaries. Come back to this section later.

WILD QUESTIONS

You've heard the term autopilot? In relationships it

means you're going through the motions. In healthy relationships, there's nothing wrong with being on autopilot sometimes. It saves time and energy. Like when you're with your best friend and you don't even have to ask if you're going to get together after school, or what to order at the coffee shop. But when the relationship is causing pain, going through the motions all but guarantees that the pain will continue. For example, if your parent is overinvolved in your life and can't stop asking about your homework or test scores, you can probably feel the question coming—along with your knee-jerk reaction—as soon as there's a quiet moment.

To break these patterns, try asking something out of the ordinary, like "What did you want to be when you were my age?" Or "If you could live anywhere in the world, where would you choose?"

Sounds easy, and it is. It works too.

Asking wild questions is a great way to shut off the autopilot function. Basically, it's a pattern interrupter. The cool thing about it is it works on multiple levels, and your parent isn't likely to recognize any of them. First, it changes the subject from something you don't want to talk about (e.g., your grades or your choice of friends) to a topic of *your* choice. Second, it forces your parents to let go of their usual behavior and consider something new. And third, it paves the way for you to share something about yourself—assuming that you want to— and to learn something new about your parents.

Other wild questions

If you could only eat one kind of food for the rest of your life, what would it be?

When you forget a thought, where does it go?

What's the most ridiculous fact you know?

If you could go back in time to a different decade or era, what would it be? What would you do? Who would you bring with you?

If you were stranded on an island and could bring three things, what would they be?

What's the dumbest/silliest movie or TV show you still love?

If you could have a superpower, what would it be, and what would you use it to do?

Who was a friend you've lost touch with that you wouldn't mind hearing from again?

If you could have any kind of job in the world and you didn't have to worry about experience or money, what would it be?

You get the idea. A final note about wild questions: If you still think this is silly, keep in mind that many adults are constantly bored and haven't had fun or goofed around in a very long time. Asking them to reconnect—through out-of-the-blue questions—with a long-forgotten part of themselves can be surprisingly effective and revealing.

Troubleshooting

Maybe your parents answer your wild question but in a way that circles back to a painful point in your relationship. Here's a good example: "My favorite car was a Mustang, but I had to get rid of it when you were born. Too hard to get a baby seat in and out of a two-door. And now I get to drive a super cool mini-van. Lucky me!"

If you get a response like this, it means your parent is stuck. Maybe they're feeling sorry for themselves. Maybe they want you to feel guilty. Maybe they miss the good old days when they were younger and less inhibited. But the reason doesn't really matter, because you're not playing that game.

You're playing the game in which you deliberately—but in a fun and creative way—disrupt old patterns and force them into a new approach. In this case, try saying something like, "Yeah, but let's say the minivan is gone and you've got twenty thousand bucks to buy whatever you want. Just for you. Do you get another Mustang or something different?" If they still won't play along, let it go and try again another time.

CHECK-IN

If you've read this chapter and still don't know where to start, that's okay. Take as much time as you need to think about it. Or read on and circle back later.

This is especially good to do if the thought of trying one of the skills makes you anxious or afraid. Trust your instincts and don't feel pressured to make quick changes.

TAKING CARE OF YOURSELF

SMALL DOSES OF SELFISHNESS

If you've learned to put your parents' feelings first, it can be hard to focus on yourself. You may have been putting others' needs ahead of your own for so many years that you've forgotten what your own needs even are. Or, worse, maybe you've convinced yourself that you don't have needs, or that you only deserve to have just a couple of your most basic needs met. Or maybe you do occasionally take a few minutes for yourself—to watch TV, play a video game, or hang out with friends—and are promptly criticized for being lazy or selfish.

If your parents are overinvolved or controlling, they may have scheduled your time so aggressively that you've forgotten what you enjoy doing. Or maybe they've told you exactly what you should and shouldn't like doing.

The messaging you've received in all of these cases is that your needs don't matter. *You* don't matter.

Not only is this not true, but it also doesn't make sense. It's fundamentally illogical. A good way to do a reality check on this one is to answer the question "How would you advise a friend in the same situation? Would you go along with their distorted view that they don't deserve to have any of their needs met? That they can't focus on themselves even for a short period of time?" Of course not. So why, then, is it acceptable for you?

The challenge of *small doses of selfishness* is that you may be so out of practice that you don't know what you want. Many teens I talk to go blank when I ask them, especially if they're struggling with symptoms of anxiety and depression. "I don't know," they'll say. "I'm not really interested in much right now." Or "I can't think of anything. I guess I'm not very interesting." Or "I'm too stressed out and overwhelmed to think of having fun."

If this is you, don't worry. All it takes to move

forward is a little detective work. What did you used to enjoy doing? What do your friends and siblings enjoy? What might you like if you were free to try it without having to worry about being judged or feeling guilty? If you still can't come up with anything, ask "If I had a free day, or even a couple of hours to myself, how would I fill it?"

There are two big takeaways here. First, you deserve to have time for yourself. It's not selfish; it's part of taking care of yourself. Second, doing so is actually a skill that needs to be practiced. If it feels weird at first, that's okay. Keep practicing. If unpleasant emotions come up—like guilt, shame, or worry about what your parents might be thinking—acknowledge the feelings but don't let them push you around. Keep practicing and you'll get better at it.

Troubleshooting

You've tried but can't stop thinking about how much work there is to do. You should be productive instead of focusing on yourself. Or you should be taking care of your parents' needs. Whatever the reason, acknowledge it and remember it. Next time, before you start your small dose of selfishness, say, "I know I'm going to feel guilty/lazy/self-involved, but that's okay. I'm going to do it anyway because it's important to take better care of myself."

Maybe you did something just for you and it was no fun at all. You didn't enjoy it and are starting to think, "I'm not that kind of person. I don't like anything." Believe it or not, for some people, doing nice things for themselves is hard work. If that's you, keep at it. Consider it an acquired skill that needs practice.

QUESTION MYTHS AND FALSE BELIEFS

Some of our cultural beliefs about parents are not true. Or maybe they're true for some people but not you. If your parents criticize you mercilessly—which makes you feel stupid, ashamed, and unloved—it would be very confusing to hear others say things like "Family is the most important thing in the world," and "Parents make mistakes, but always with the best of intentions."

Learning to question these beliefs can take some of the power away from them. It can also relieve you of the responsibility of trying to make sense of things that don't fit with your experiences. Instead of saying "All parents love their children, so it must be my fault if I don't feel loved," you'll say "All parents love their children? Really? That doesn't fit with my experience. It's not true for me."

Here are some exaggerated or false beliefs that you might hear from your friends, at school, on TV and the internet, from your parents and grandparents, etc. Put a check next to any you believe, or that you've been told—directly or indirectly—are true:

_____ All parents love their children.

_____ Family is the most important thing.

_____ Your parents will always love you,
no matter what.

_____ If parents hurt their children and cause
them emotional pain, they're doing it
for their children's own good.

_____ Having few emotional needs is a sign
of strength.

_____ You can talk to your parents about anything.

_____ Your parents will always be there for you.

_____ You can always trust your parents.

_____ It's your job to honor and respect your parents no matter how they treat you.

_____ Your parents only want what's best for you.

_____ Your parents know more than you do.

The problem with these statements is they're distortions of reality. Take, for example, "Having few emotional needs is a strength." While this could be a short-term strategy, it's not healthy or ideal. The long-term consequences of learning to get by with minimal care for your emotional needs are terrible. And unnecessary.

Go ahead and pick one of the myths you checked.

Write it out in your notebook (or the margins of this book), and explain how you came to believe this myth. Is it something your parent told you? Is it something you've observed in other families? Is it something you came to on your own to try to make sense of your experiences?

Next, rewrite the myth so it fits your actual experiences. We're looking for reality here. *Your* reality, not what your parents or other people think.

Lastly, read your rewritten version out loud. Does this version change what you think or how you feel? If so, expand it with as much detail as you can. Does it give you any clues about how you'd like to live and be treated by others in the future? Write down those insights too.

DEAL WITH YOUR ANGER

You just finished thinking about some of the false beliefs about parents. When you hear these myths enough, you start to believe them. In your mind, they change from an idea to a fact. And when those "facts" differ from your actual experiences, this creates a big conflict inside of you.

Here's an example. In your head you think, "Children are always supposed to love and respect their parents, but I'm feeling mad at them. And if I'm feeling mad at them, that means I'm ungrateful/ not a good person. I don't want to be a bad person, so maybe I'm just stressed. I'll go to my room and hide out for a while until I feel better."

You're probably not even aware of this process when it happens. You don't actually think it through, step by step. But over time you learn to see anger as an unacceptable emotion. You become afraid of what it might mean about you as a person. Or how others might judge you if they experience it. So you try to hide it. Or push it away. Or bury it. Or suppress it by using alcohol, drugs, food, tech distractions, etc.

Some of these strategies work, but at best they're short-term fixes. Swallowing anger comes at a big cost—to your mental health, relationships, and even, potentially, your physical health. But there's another, bigger cost: denial of your true self. When you're angry but can't allow yourself to acknowledge and express it, you start to lose touch with who you really are.

The fix is pretty clear, however, as the steps below show:

Give yourself permission to be angry. Tell yourself, "It's okay: I have every right to feel this way. I have reasons to be angry, and those reasons are _____, _____, and _____. Anyone living through the same experiences would feel angry too. My anger is a logical response. It doesn't mean anything about me as a person, and it certainly doesn't mean anything bad about me."

Notice and express your anger. Anger is an emotional response, sure, but it's also physical. Where do you feel it in your body? What does it feel like? Sit with it for a moment and then say to yourself, "I know I'm angry right now because I feel it in my chest/shoulders/jaw. Again, I'm angry because _____. And when I feel this way, I really want to _____."

Don't worry about the rightness or wrongness of what you write, and try not to be frightened by it. Write it on a piece of scrap paper and throw it away when you're done, if that makes it easier. Journal about it or discuss it with your therapist, if you have one. The point is to find some way to express your anger instead of hiding it or suppressing it.

Use your anger. Anger has a powerful energetic component. It's a bit like nuclear fission: If you split an atom, a tremendous amount of energy is released. You can use this energy to power cities or blow things up. Take a moment to think about what you might put your energy into. The obvious examples are all things artistic or athletic, but the possibilities are endless. Write down how you might use your anger, instead of bottling it up or explaining it away.

One warning here is to avoid confronting others when you're angry. The intensity of emotion basically shuts off (temporarily) the functions needed to communicate effectively.

Become curious about the meaning of your anger. This isn't a silver linings kind of thing where I'm asking you to look on the bright side. Or to reframe bad things in your life as a gift. This is a way of saying that, after you've acknowledged and expressed your anger, you can disconnect it from your identity and look at it more closely, differently.

To put it another way, give yourself the freedom to be angry at your parents without it meaning anything about you—as a son, daughter, child, or human being. And if it doesn't mean anything about you as a person, you can look at flareups of anger as information. Cues that your boundaries are being crossed or ignored. You can learn to detach a little and observe your anger.

DEAL WITH YOUR GRIEF

A curious thing happens when some people deal with their anger over how they've been treated: They discover that underneath that anger, or along with it, is grief. Not the kind of grief that happens when someone close to you dies. I'm talking about the kind that accompanies the loss of certain hopes, ideas, or fantasies. Maybe you feel as if you've lost your childhood or adolescence, or maybe it's the feeling that you missed out on having a normal one. Maybe you've lost your self-respect or self-esteem, your feeling of safety, or your trust in adults. The thing I hear most often from teens is grief over the loss of their innocence.

One of the reasons people avoid facing these thoughts is because the grief that goes along with them is so painful. It might show up as anger, rage, sadness, shock, doubt, or confusion. Many of us will do just about anything to avoid these feelings. Like pretending we're okay when we're not. Or pretending that it never happened.

The problem, as I'm sure you're learning by now, is that avoidance and pretending are only effective for one thing: allowing the hurtful behavior to continue. Beginning on page 137, you will learn a powerful technique—setting and holding boundaries—for stopping your parents' hurtful behavior. But for now let's talk about how to deal with grief.

First, know that grief is a normal response under these circumstances. Acknowledge it and talk about it to a trusted friend, sibling, or therapist. If you're worried that what you have to say is too intense for others to hear, write it out in your journal. A good script is:

"It's like I've lost _____ and this is how it makes me feel: _____ ."

Finally, practice radical acceptance. You do this by letting go and saying it out loud, to yourself, when no one else is around. "I am officially letting go of having the perfect family/making my parents happy/having a normal childhood. It's better for me to live in reality and be true to myself and my actual feelings." Sometimes saying this out loud can be a tremendous relief. For many, however, it can release powerful other emotions. Remind yourself that all your feelings are valid, and that grief changes with time and doesn't last forever.

STOP MAKING EXCUSES FOR YOUR PARENTS

Let's say you have a friend over and your parents are rude and sarcastic. Or your mom has been drinking. She's in the same room as you and your friend and is acting like a teen herself, saying inappropriate and embarrassing things. You might be tempted to defend your mom's behavior and try to explain it. "She doesn't mean it. She's not usually like this."

There are several problems with making excuses. First, it's a reversal of roles that puts you in the parental position. But because you're not the parent, you don't have the power to do anything about it. Can you imagine saying, in the above example, "You're drunk and acting inappropriately. Go to your room and don't come out until you sober up and act your age!" It sounds ridiculous and it is. That's the point.

It's also a problem because, when you make excuses, you're giving the green light for the behavior to continue. In effect, you're saying, "Go on and do whatever. I'll be here to clean up any mess you leave behind."

Lastly, making excuses for your parents' bad behavior discounts your own feelings. If you're hurt or offended by someone else's behavior, you shouldn't have to come up with a reason. Doing so says, "My feelings don't matter. What matters is that I don't confront the behavior and risk upsetting them." You're saying that their feelings are more important than your own. This is never true.

So, what to do about it? The first step is to figure out why, exactly, you're excusing their behavior. Here are some common reasons:

Loyalty: If you've been taught to believe things like

family is everything, and *it's not okay to share family secrets*, calling out your parents' behavior for what it is might be seen as disloyal. *You* might be seen as disloyal.

Fear of rejection: This threat carries real weight in a family and is often enough to get teens to justify or rationalize their parents' problem behaviors.

Shame: If the behaviors in question are especially ugly and scary to you, it can feel embarrassing or shameful to let others see it. Making excuses protects your story of a happy family.

Hopelessness: Maybe you've given up on improving your situation. Making excuses feels false, but what else are you going to do?

Tolerance: It's been happening your whole life and now seems normal.

Next, forgive yourself for having made excuses. You did it to get by, not to ruin your self-esteem.

Now that you've figured out the reason behind

the excuses, you can stop doing it. It's not likely that this will prompt a change in your parents' behavior, but it's still worth doing. It keeps you connected to reality, and brings you closer to your true self. Let's go through the five most common excuses.

Loyalty: Remind yourself that loyalty has nothing to do with excusing inappropriate or hurtful behavior. You can show loyalty to your family in positive ways that feel good to you.

Fear of rejection: If you acted badly, would you expect family members to make excuses for you? If your parents refused to do so, would you threaten to reject them? Of course not. You can hold your parents to a similar standard. Belonging in your family should never be dependent on your silence.

Shame: Writer and shame researcher Brené Brown has said that shame needs secrecy, silence, and judgment to grow. I'd argue that making excuses is a form of silence. You're silencing your own emotions. If you speak up, what will happen? Maybe your parents will have to face the consequences of their behavior. Even if they don't, you get to use your voice. This is a step toward taking control over your life.

Hopelessness: If the situation with your parents truly feels hopeless, maybe it's time to seek meaningful connection outside your family. Pay special attention to the chapter *Beyond Your Parents* beginning on page 176.

Tolerance: This may sound like a bumper sticker, but what can be learned can be unlearned. Start paying attention to other relationships in which people treat each other better.

TAKING AND LEAVING RESPONSIBILITY

I often hear from teens that they feel overwhelmed by too many responsibilities. They have too much on their plate but are afraid of letting anything go because it might mean that they're lazy, or not meeting expectations. Keep in mind that there are limits to what even the most conscientious and productive person can do. It's okay to restructure your life into the responsibilities that make sense for you to do and those that are unrealistic or just plain not important to you. This is a great exercise to do when you're too wiped out for heavy emotional work. It's very concrete and practical.

First, make a list of the things you will start or continue to take responsibility for.

Below are a few examples, but feel free to include whatever makes sense for you:

• Owning my feelings and actually feeling them

• Asking for help when I need it (including outside the family, such as talking to a school social worker or counselor)

• Trying my best in school

• Keeping my room clean

• Getting up on time, on my own

• Helping with household chores

Second, make a list of the things you will NOT take responsibility for. Again, these are just examples:

• My parents' bad behavior

• My parents' stress, unhappiness, or other difficult emotions

• My parents' money, career, or marriage problems

• The burden of getting my parents to change

• Figuring out a way to get my parents to love me

BECOME AN OBSERVER

This is a strategy to use when you're in the middle of a conflict. *Becoming an observer* is the opposite of being reactive. It's what happens when you take a step back and mentally record everything that's going on in the interaction: what your parents are saying, how they're saying it, and what it might mean. Also, what you're thinking and feeling, as well as what you feel compelled to do or say.

Why should you become an observer? Because it's hard to think clearly and make good decisions when you're emotional. When you step back even a little bit, you may be able to see things differently. It's like widening a camera's focus. Simply put, you see more. If you're wondering "What is there to see? They're saying stuff that's wrong and makes me mad," the answer is, "A lot." What's going on between you and your parents in an argument is actually quite complex. But don't worry: I'm not going to bore you with a detailed autopsy of a parent-teen argument. What I *will* do is walk you through the steps of how to get space during an argument and not get pushed around by your thoughts and feelings.

Describe the situation to yourself. Be as specific as possible. "I'm in the living room, getting ready to go out with my friends. And my dad is blocking the doorway because he doesn't want me to go. He's giving me the same lecture I've heard a hundred times, and he doesn't know what he's talking about." If you push yourself a little further, you might come up with this: "What's really going on, though, is my mom's pissed at him and went to stay with her sister, and he hates that. So he's taking it out on me because it's Friday night and I have plans and he's going to be stuck home alone feeling sorry for himself."

Label your thoughts and emotions. Try to be accurate rather than judgmental. Are you angry, sad, ashamed, surprised, shocked, disgusted? What are you thinking? "I'm thinking it's not my problem, but he's trying to *make* it my problem." "I'm thinking of walking out the door and leaving. What's he going to do, ground me?"

What's going on physically in your body? Are you dizzy? Shaking? Is there tension or a feeling of tightness in your chest, neck, jaw, shoulders, or back? Do you feel exhausted or drained? Distracted? Foggy? Is your heart beating fast? Whatever it is, just label it.

Ask yourself this: "While I'm having these thoughts and feelings, do I absolutely have to act right now? What would happen if I did nothing?"

It takes practice to learn to become an observer. Try it first when things are relatively calm. You might find that in the course of working through the four steps, you become distracted. This is okay. The goal in a conflict is to lower the intensity of emotion; it's much harder to experience intense emotions and react to them when you're distracted.

DEAL WITH THE SITUATION INSTEAD OF THE RELATIONSHIP

Full disclosure: This may be the hardest skill in the book to learn and use. It's also the one with the greatest potential to improve your life. Why? Because it reframes the goal from fixing or changing your parents to the simpler, more manageable goal of getting the most out of any particular situation. And by *getting the most*, I mean a) meeting your needs, b) staying true to yourself, and c) being respectful in the same way you want others to be respectful to you.

Getting the most does not mean trying to save or fix your family, pretending that everything is okay when it's not, or trying to earn your parents' love by working too hard or denying your own needs. If the difference isn't clear, it will be when you read the situations below.

JESSICA

Jessica, who has never played a sport in her life, has decided to join the softball team. It's her senior year, and she wants to experience being an athlete. The only problem is the school requires a current physical and she's way overdue. She has mentioned it several times to her father, who is hopelessly distracted by his job and generally uninvolved in her life. When she expressed disappointment, her father got angry and said, "You want to try paying the bills and keeping track of your and your brothers' activities? I didn't think so."

In this case, Jessica's need is for her father to be more organized and reliable. Organized in this case means keeping track of the basic medical needs of his kids, which includes annual physicals. Reliable means that if he says he'll do something— especially something important like meeting the requirements for Jessica to play softball—he will follow through. The problem is, Jessica can't make her father more organized. She can't make him more reliable. But she *can* deal with the specific situation. What would this look like? Let's see.

Dealing with the situation

Since this scenario is based on a real person, I'll tell you what the real Jessica did. She went to the school nurse and explained what was going on. She was tempted to out her father as a hopeless flake whom she couldn't count on for anything, but instead she stayed focused on the situation at hand. She explained how important it was for her to join the softball team and that her father wasn't able to help at the moment.

The results were positive. The nurse told Jessica that, because of the district-wide deadline, local pediatricians' offices were too booked, but urgent care centers were picking up the slack. They required only one day's notice, which worked out well: Jessica scheduled the appointment herself, and the next day, her father agreed to drive her there and sign her in using his insurance card.

What's important about this example is that Jessica didn't waste energy or emotion trying to change her father. She was never going to make him more organized or reliable, so she focused on getting her needs met. She was realistic about what he could and couldn't do and recruited him to play a small but critical role. You might argue that she took on too much adult responsibility, but that was just the reality of her situation. She did a nice job of working with her reality while focusing on getting her needs met. In terms of the three guidelines for *getting the most* out of the situation, she met her own needs, stayed true to herself, and was respectful.

ROBERT

Robert is frustrated because his mom insists on knowing where he is at all times. He has been planning a day-long bike trip with his friends, and his mother is insisting on check-ins every thirty minutes, downloading a tracking app on his phone, and a bike shop safety inspection, despite the fact that Robert is an excellent mechanic and has put a lot of time and effort into getting his gear ready. She has been intruding on Robert's privacy for years, barging into his room, and giving him weekly task lists for school and college planning.

In this case, Robert feels that his mother is treating him like a little kid and that her behavior is far too intense and intrusive. She doesn't trust him and thinks he'll make bad decisions if she isn't around to tell him exactly what to do. He wants to tell her that this kind of behavior is inappropriate and that he's too old for such a level of supervision. His fear, however, is that she'll become even more controlling and start calling his friends' parents, possibly to try to cancel the trip.

Dealing with the situation

With the date of the trip approaching, Robert lets go of the goal of changing his mother. He focuses instead on getting her to back off enough so he can enjoy his time with his friends. In the school library, he prints a copy of his route. He gives it to his mother and says, "I'm a very trustworthy and responsible person, and I want to start managing my own time and looking out for myself, starting with this trip. I know this might be hard for you, so I'll send a text when we stop for lunch, and again when we finish the ride. Thanks for understanding and for agreeing not to call or text me while I'm riding, since that could be dangerous."

Did Robert's mother like this plan? No, but she followed it. What I appreciate about it is how clearly Robert articulated his need (to manage his own time and be independent), and how he included the bit at the end about not calling or texting. Did this stop his mother from trying to micromanage his life after the ride? Absolutely not, but that wasn't his goal. He knew he'd have to set and uphold new boundaries with his mother throughout the rest of his life. Taking it one situation at a time made the effort bearable.

CARMEN

Carmen feels like she has tolerated her father's criticisms for too long. Nothing she does is good enough, and his hurtful comments have taken a toll on her mood and self-esteem. She has discussed it at length with her therapist, who has suggested the possibility that Carmen's father never received love or support from his own demanding parents and thus fears emotional closeness with his daughter. Her therapist has encouraged Carmen to have a heart-to-heart conversation with him, but Carmen has never done this and is afraid her father will lose his temper and talk right over her.

After a particularly hurtful comment from him about her best friend, Carmen decides she has to do something. She summons her courage and says to her father, "You're mean and you hate everyone. Why can't you just love me?" Her father answers, "You think I'm mean, but everything I'm doing is for your own good. You don't know how the world is. You don't know how people are. Do you think my parents gave me hugs and kisses and told me everything was going to be fine? No, because they were working too damned hard, and they knew what would happen if they told me lies and pretended that the world was going to give me a fair shake . . ."

Dealing with the situation

Carmen talked it over with her therapist and figured something out: She was never going to get her father to change. That was too big a goal. But maybe she could express herself and get him to listen. She wrote this out on a piece of paper and read it to him the next day: "Dad, I just want you to listen and not say anything after. What you said about my friend Julia really hurt my feelings. I know you don't like her family, but she's important to me."

What's great about Carmen's goal is that it was small enough to be achievable, and personal enough to be meaningful. Also, it didn't require anything from her father other than for him to listen. He was able to do that. Carmen was happy with the outcome, and for the first time in her relationship with her father, she felt the beginnings of confidence. Instead of feeling diminished and belittled, she had expressed herself and was heard.

It's very important to note that, in this last case, Carmen's father did not understand his daughter any better. He didn't become less mean, or more empathetic. And it's tempting to say "Big deal. All he did was listen." But that was exactly what Carmen wanted from the situation. Similarly, Robert's mother didn't mellow out or give him more space in his life. But she did respect his boundaries around his bike trip, which was exactly what he wanted.

CHECK-IN

This chapter may bring up intense emotions like sadness and anger. Give yourself time to sit with whatever feelings come up. Don't judge them as bad or wrong, and don't think you need to force a change right away. If the feelings persist, try journaling or talking to a trusted friend or a therapist. You can also take a break from reading and come back when you're ready. Most of all, remember that it's okay to feel this way and you're already doing great work by reading and thinking about this chapter.

SETTING GOOD BOUNDARIES

In simple terms, boundaries are limits you set and share with your parents (and others). Boundaries let people know what to say and what not to say when they're around you. What to do and not do. They also let others know what you are and are not responsible for.

Boundaries are truly amazing. When you learn how to set them—and hold them when others continue to overstep, as they do—your relationships get better. Your mental health will improve, too, along with your self-esteem. It's hard not to feel better about yourself when you say what you need and are listened to.

You've probably heard about boundaries before but don't know exactly how to create them. You're not alone. Honestly, most adults don't know either. They don't know when boundaries are needed or how to set them. And they certainly don't know how to teach you about them.

Another reason you may not have learned about boundaries is because, as a culture, we avoid conflict. This isn't apparent in the world of social media, of course. But if you spend time with as many families as I do, it's clear: People will do almost anything—including giving up on their own emotional needs—to avoid conflict with those they are close to. It's a shame, because setting boundaries isn't rocket science, and it's one of those skills that keeps paying off throughout the rest of your life.

If you're thinking, "Wait. I already know what my boundaries are but no one follows them," it's a fair point. But it's not enough for you to know. Your parents need to know too. Remember the line from the beginning of the book about people being really bad at reading minds? It applies especially to boundaries. From now on, it's going to be up to you to let your parents know what your boundaries are and what you'll do if they overstep or refuse to respect them.

Let's go over boundary rules, and then we'll dig into some sample scripts.

BOUNDARY RULES

The first rule in setting boundaries is to be clear. Very clear. Crystal clear. A lot of people associate this with being mean, grumpy, selfish, or controlling. It's none of these things. It's just good communication. There's nothing mean about saying "I don't want to talk about my body or weight at the dinner table." It's specific, and it's about what you need. There's nothing nasty or selfish about saying "I can't return your texts right away when I'm in class because I need to focus on school."

Boundaries are NOT used to make your parents change or to control them. They're to let your parents know what *you'll* do if they continue talking or acting in ways that are hurtful or make you uncomfortable.

When you set a boundary, keep it short and speak in a calm, even tone. Don't argue or negotiate.

It's okay if your parents don't agree with your boundary or your reasons for it. They don't even need to understand it, as long as they recognize and accept it. If they can do this, they're showing respect for you and your needs. Even if they still believe that you're wrong.

Don't hint at your boundary or *kind of suggest* what you need. Be explicit. Don't leave it to them to infer or interpret.

Avoid setting boundaries when you're angry. Setting boundaries isn't about getting even or making your parents apologize for past wrongs. It's about getting your needs met. If you're feeling a lot of anger, deal with it directly. (Page 114 will help.)

Be firm and respectful. This doesn't mean you need to be excessively polite and overly concerned with your parents' emotions. It's okay if they feel upset or hurt for a while. It's *their* business to sit with and process those feelings; not yours.

As hard as it might be, don't apologize, explain, or negotiate. This may feel weird the first few times. Practice setting a boundary when no one is around, or with a trusted sibling or friend. Write it on a piece of paper and read it word for word. Practice until it comes out smoothly. If you're still not sure of yourself, bring the paper with you and read it aloud.

Start your boundary journey with small stuff. Get one or two easy ones under your belt before you try the ones that are most important to you.

If you miss your moment to set or hold a boundary, it's okay. You can come back to it later. If your parents say, "But that was days ago," you can say, "I know, but it's still important to me, which is why I'm bringing it up now." Or "It's been on my mind, and I need to address it now."

Don't switch arguments or bring up other behaviors. You want to keep it clear and simple. One thing at a time.

If you or your parents get too emotional, table the conversation. Say, "Let's talk about this another time." If you're worried your parents will never want to talk about it again, say something like "Let's pick this up tomorrow, after dinner."

Words matter a lot here, so be thoughtful about the ones you choose. Avoid saying "always" and "never." Use "and" in place of "but." And be careful not to begin your boundary statements with "unfortunately." Using words like these shows you're nervous about your parents' possible discomfort. The unfortunate thing is that the boundary is probably long overdue!

SAMPLE SCRIPTS

Below are suggested conversational approaches to ten of the most common boundary problems. This is the only part of the book where I encourage you to read the entire chapter, even if some of the problems don't apply to you and your parents. The reason is because the skill of setting boundaries is dependent on language. Reading all of the samples is good exposure to the style and words that work best.

For each sample, we will begin with a description of the problematic parent behavior. After that, there will be a boundary statement you can use. Feel free to improvise, change, or add to these statements to personalize them; they'll work best if they fit the way you yourself talk. (By the way, this is a good place to mark up your book. Circle the ones you want to try. Write margin notes for things to add or change.)

After each boundary statement, we'll deal with pressure points, which in this case means pushback. You should expect a certain amount of pushback, especially at the beginning. Some people get frustrated or angry when they deliver a beautifully clear boundary statement and get resistance. It's normal, especially if your parents are used to you quietly tolerating their behavior.

Instead of seeing pushback as disrespect, you can reframe it as uncertainty on the part of your parents. You're changing the rules in the family. Your parents aren't sure how to react to it. *Do you really mean it? Is this for real?* Yes, you mean it, and the pushback section will show you exactly what to say.

It is frustrating to have to restate or refine a boundary, but keep in mind that some parents are going to need more time and repetition than others. I've heard of cases where months after a teen set a boundary, their parent caught themselves in the middle of a hurtful comment and said, "Oh, right. I'm not supposed to talk that way around you." If this happens to you, you might be tempted to say something like "Yes, and I've only been telling you for three months!" Resist the urge, however difficult it might be. Even if it comes late, it's still progress. You might even want to say thank you. See page 96 about *Catching Good.*

CRITICISM AND PUT-DOWNS

Let's say your parents are constantly putting you down. They never miss an opportunity to tell you how much they dislike your friends, fashion choices, or work ethic. They're also vocal about how much time you spend in your room. It's starting to affect your mood and self-esteem, which in turn leads you to isolate even more.

Boundary statement

"Thanks, but I'm not really looking for opinions." It's tempting to say "... not looking for opinions *right now*," but I wouldn't. Some parents will take that to mean that your boundary is temporary, as in *they can't say mean things today, but tomorrow it will be back to normal.*

Pushback

Often a parent will justify their unwanted comments by telling you their motive, which may be worry, fear of you making a bad choice that might affect your future, or even love. As in, "Honey, we're not criticizing. We're just worried about you and your future. We don't want to see you go down the wrong path." Your response? "I know you're worried about me, but saying things like that doesn't help. Thanks for understanding." Thanking them may seem unnecessarily polite, but it's not. You're applying a little pressure of your own and thanking them in advance for respecting your needs in the future. A shorter, simpler response is, "I know you're saying it out of love, but I've got this." What I like about this one is that it's a clear statement of confidence. *You* are in charge of the decisions that your parents have been questioning.

INTRUSIVE BEHAVIOR

Maybe your parents snoop on your phone when it's left unlocked. Or they track your location when you're out and tell you it's for your safety, in case of an accident. Or they barge into your room without knocking. Whatever the situation, you're feeling like your privacy is being invaded.

Boundary statement
"Please don't go in my room/look through my

phone/track my location. I want us to be able to trust each other." Or "Please knock before you come in. I really need privacy in here."

Pushback

This can be a complicated one, especially if it's a cell phone issue and your parents are paying the bill. But it really isn't about money. It's about your right to privacy, and it's about trust. Stay focused on those two things. If your parent says, "Too bad. It's my house and I make the rules," say, "True, but I still need some privacy. Thanks for understanding and respecting that. It means a lot to me." I'd make this an absolute with your bedroom and the bathroom. Resist the urge to ask "Why don't you trust me?" or "What do I have to do to convince you that I can be trusted?" You shouldn't have to jump through hoops or negotiate for a basic right.

CONTROLLING BEHAVIOR

Even though you're old enough to drive and have a job, maybe your parents are still managing and controlling every aspect of your life, from daily activities to the classes you take, what you eat, college planning, etc. Maybe you're feeling increasingly stressed and overwhelmed, and you're no longer sure you're even interested in your activities.

You asked your parents if you could drop a class and an extracurricular so you could relax and enjoy being a teenager, but they became very upset and launched into a big guilt trip about how hard they've been working to help you become successful, and how much they've sacrificed.

Boundary statement

"Thanks for helping, but I think it's time I make my own decisions around school and activities." Or "I'm ready to be more independent and want to plan my own schedule for next semester." Or "Thanks for the reminders about the early admission deadline and requirements, but I'm on it."

Pushback

Your parents listen attentively to your boundary statement. After a long and awkward silence, they say, "Do you remember what happened last year when you got behind in two of your classes? You would have failed if we hadn't gotten involved. You've worked too hard to risk something like that." Your response? "I know you want me to be successful. I want that too, and I'm going to start by picking my own classes."

Keep in mind that the real problem has little to do with your classes or success. The real problem is your parents' lack of separation. They see you as an extension of themselves, equating your mistakes and failures with their own. And they'll go to great lengths to reduce the risk of failure . . . even if it harms your relationship.

The good news is you don't have to fix this. Whether or not they can separate their identify from yours is up to them. *You* will be responsible, however, for drawing lines. "I know the essay is important, but it's my responsibility and I will write it myself." "I'm aware of the deadline and I'll finish the application. If I don't get it done, I'll deal with the consequences."

UNWANTED OBSERVATIONS AND ADVICE

Whether the comments are about your health, body, fashion, relationships, politics, grades, college choices, or just about anything, having your parents give you unwanted advice can really drive a wedge between you. Or widen an existing divide. Your parents may believe that they're trying to help, but the reality is you don't need or want their advice. Or maybe you're open to advice, but not from them.

The key feature here is that the information or judgment is unwanted. You didn't ask. The comments and attention feel uncomfortable or even painful. You've given your parents lots of cues, but they're not getting it. "You're still friends with him?" "Are you really going to eat that?" "You know what you should do? I'll tell you . . ." "You're not going to wear those pants, are you?"

Boundary statement

"Thanks, but I'm in charge of my hair/fashion/whatever."

"I'm good. Let's change the subject." Or "I'd rather not talk about my weight/relationships/grades/etc."

If you'd like something even stronger, say, "Please don't talk about my hair/fashion/whatever in front of me. It makes me uncomfortable." Or "I'd appreciate it if we can skip the diet talk. Thanks." Or "Please stop giving me advice about this."

Pushback

Expect to hear things like "We know what's best for you," "We just want you to be happy/avoid mistakes/be successful," "You're too young to understand," and "You'll thank us later, when you're older." They might tell you that the world is a hard place and they "just want you to be prepared," or that they want to help you be the best possible version of yourself. And if none of these are effective, they may resort to guilt and tell you, "We've sacrificed so much for you. We have a right to express our opinion."

In any of these cases, you can say, "Thanks for caring, but I'm going to make my own decisions." You might have to repeat it a few times for them to get the message. If they're still not hearing you, try saying,

"I know you're trying to help me, but I'm telling you what I need: to stop talking about this." Or "Please let me take care of my own hair/clothes/body. I've got it."

RACIST, HOMOPHOBIC, OR OTHER DISCRIMINATORY TALK

Your parents are aware of your views about their bigotry, but they continue using intolerant and hurtful language in your presence. Or maybe they're not aware because you've kept your feelings to yourself, suspecting that they wouldn't listen to you anyway. Or maybe they'd go so far as to make fun of you for objecting.

Boundary statement

"What you're saying (or how you're saying it) isn't okay. You should stop now." If they continue, then you can say, "I'm going to leave now because I don't want to hear homophobic/racist/ableist talk like that." It can be especially good to name the behavior or language, but don't spend a lot of energy trying to change your parent's perceptions or political views.

Remember, setting a boundary is about expressing your limits and not about changing other people. Ideally, they will respond positively with something like, "Well, I didn't know I was being racist, and I'll definitely change." But such responses are rare. For now, it's enough if they get the message that they can't talk that way in front of you.

Pushback

Depending on how strong your parents' beliefs are, you may hear comments like "You don't know what you're talking about," and "Stop being so sensitive." As hard as it might be, resist arguing or explaining. Be clear about what it is you can no longer tolerate. "It makes me feel bad when you say homophobic things." "I can't stay in this conversation if you keep making racist comments." If your parents push back with "We're just joking around," say, "It's not funny. It's racist. Please stop." If they persist, excuse yourself.

Some teens have asked, "If I give up on changing my parents' minds, isn't that the same as enabling? Doesn't that make me part of the problem?" It's a great question. First, you don't have to give up on them. You should, however, take care of your needs in the present. If you give up on *that*—to wade into the misery of a heated argument or yet another soul-draining explanation of your position—you haven't helped anyone. Second, setting and holding boundaries with your parents on offensive behavior is a brave and noble thing to do.

MISGENDERING

You've told your parents many times that, as a trans and gender nonconforming (TGNC) person, your pronouns are they/them (or other pronouns or combination of pronouns). They continue to call you *she/her*, even though other family members have made the shift.

Boundary statement

"My pronouns are they/them. Please remember next time." If you need something stronger, try "When you call me *she*, it's hard for me to feel close to you." You could say "Stop calling me that!" but remember that you can't make anyone do anything, so it's useful to establish a connection between correct pronouns and being able to have a close relationship.

If they can't comply, the result shouldn't come as a surprise to them.

Pushback

Maybe your parents act like they're the hurt party and say, "We've been calling you the same thing for sixteen years. It's going to take us a while, so be patient." Or "We're old. Give us a break." Or "Relax. Don't be so sensitive." Your response? "Mom, Dad, when you call me the wrong name, it really hurts. I want to spend time with you, but I can't if you keep calling me by the wrong name."

This paves the way for the next step, which is to limit your time around them. I know this gets tricky when you're dependent on your parents for many things. But you have to take care of your needs, and that might involve keeping things businesslike and skipping family time. Without feeling guilty about it. That's a type of boundary setting as well.

UNRELIABLE BEHAVIOR

Let's say your parents make plans and never follow through. Or they cancel appointments and even parties or dinners that you'd like to go to. Or they just don't show up. You've talked about it a bunch of times, but they act like they have no clue, or like you're exaggerating. "That was one time," they say. Or "Hey, *you* try working my job and raising kids. If I'm late, I'm late."

There are many possible reasons for this behavior, so be as specific as possible when setting this boundary. If your parent misses most of your soccer games or shows up in the last ten minutes, build your boundary around that. If the reason is they're a single parent working two jobs, pick one game that's especially important and ask if they can commit to that.

Boundary statement

"I know you're busy, but it would mean a lot if you could be home for dinner when I'm staying at your house." Or "I appreciate how hard you work, but let's not make plans if you can't keep them."

Pushback

It's common for parents to get defensive and put this one back on you. They might say, "Why don't you do the grocery shopping and pick up your little brother? Then I'll have all the time in the world to be more punctual." Resist the temptation to argue. It's okay to offer to discuss their suggestion, but make it clear that it's a discussion for later. Right now it's about your feelings. Specifically, that you feel bad when they don't show up for you. You want to be closer, and it would go a long way if they could follow through and keep the next promise.

One more thing: If they do keep the next promise or commitment, make sure to say something about it. "Thank you for coming to the game. It means a lot."

NONSTOP NEWS AND POLITICS

Your parents have extreme political views and never miss a chance to express them. Everyone is entitled to their opinions, but the tone of their comments has become increasingly angry. Your views are very different, and you don't feel comfortable sharing them. On the few occasions you've tried, it has resulted in arguments, lectures, and rants from your parents. The last time, your father said, "Are you sure you're in the right family?" after which he gave you the cold shoulder for days.

Boundary statement

"I know we have different views on politics, so let's not bring it up. That way, we can all relax and enjoy our time together."

Pushback

Maybe you get a hard stare followed by "It's my house. If I want to talk about what's going on in this country, I will." Your response? "I respect your opinion, Dad. Please respect my decision not to talk politics. If you can't, it's going to make it hard for us to spend time together."

CONSTANT PRYING AND QUESTIONING

Your parents ask several times a day how you're feeling. If you say "Good," or "Fine," they follow up with increasingly more intrusive questions, as though you're lying or holding out. And maybe you are, but with good reason: It's none of their business! You don't want to talk about it with them and you have a good reason. Maybe it's something you've already discussed with a therapist or a close friend. Maybe it's not appropriate to discuss with parents. Or you're worried that doing so will result in a change in the relationship that you're not ready for or don't want. Another possibility is that you're okay with your mood, even if it's stormy, and don't think it's realistic to be happy and cheerful for the sake of others.

Boundary statement

"You don't have to check on my emotions all the time. I'm okay. And when I'm not, I know what to do."

Pushback

Your parents say, "We're just worried. You've seemed so depressed lately. We want you to be happy." Your reply? "Asking me about it all the time doesn't help. What helps is letting me be in charge of my own emotions. If I need help, I'll ask."

TELLING EMBARRASSING STORIES ABOUT YOU

Your parents like to overshare and tell awkward stories from your past, especially when you have company over. Maybe they think it's nostalgic, funny, or a way to relate to you. Regardless, you've hinted that you don't like it, but they're not getting the message. Now, whenever there's a family gathering or other guests are over, you sit through it with anxiety, wondering which of your worst stories they're going to share and when.

Boundary statement

"Sharing these stories doesn't feel good for me. Please talk about something else." You can invoke the same boundary if they talk about others who aren't present. Say, "I'd rather not talk about other people when they're not here. It doesn't feel right to me."

Pushback

You state your boundary and your parents say, "Lighten up. We're joking around." Your response? "I get it, but I'm telling you it's not funny. It's embarrassing and hurtful, so please stop." If they refuse, excuse yourself. If they ask where you're going, or why you're being so sensitive, say, "I just told you: This isn't good for me, so I need to leave." What you're basically saying is "While I used to sit through this stuff and feel bad for days, I'm not going to do it anymore. Either you talk about something else, or I'm out."

CHECK-IN

If you've read this chapter and are nervous about trying to set a boundary with your parents, it's okay to be cautious and wait. Boundaries are powerful tools, but trust your instincts. If your situation is too intense, back off and start with an easier skill or strategy, like Questioning Myths or Small Doses of Selfishness. You can revisit setting boundaries when things feel calmer. In the meantime, if your parents continue to overstep, notice it and think about the boundary statement you might use in the future, when you're ready.

POSITIVE CONVERSATIONS

This is the place where you're going to use several of the skills and strategies you've learned to plan a positive conversation with your parents. This isn't mandatory. You may have decided to focus on non-talking strategies. Or you may need to work up to it. Both are fine.

If you're ready to start a conversation, the discussion points and sample scripts below will help. Depending on your needs, some of these conversations will be about ordinary things like getting permission for a school trip, asking for help to set up an appointment or get a ride somewhere, or talking about what's going on in your life. Others will be about difficult subjects like your mental health, something your parents did that upset you, or some bad news you might have received.

Whatever the circumstances, here are some helpful guidelines:

- Plan to talk when it's a good time for both of you. (See "Right Time/Wrong Time", page 92)

- Don't start a conversation when you're angry, upset, or exhausted.

- Don't start a conversation before going out with friends, to work, or some other activity. You don't want to have to rush this.

- Frame the conversation with the amount of time you need. If your parents are especially defensive or unpredictable, say, "Can we talk for five minutes?" You may not realize it, but for some parents a conversation can make them anxious. They may be fearful of what you will bring up and whether they'll be able to deal with it. Don't let this dissuade you; just be clear about the time commitment you're asking for. Almost anyone can agree to five minutes.

▪ If either of you gets angry or emotional, take a break, call a time-out, and say, "I think this is a good place to stop for today."

▪ Stick to your original topic. Don't shift to other issues that might come up. If you feel like your parent is throwing other issues or situations at you and expecting a response, say, "Okay, but I want to stick to this topic.
We can talk about that other thing tomorrow."

▪ Be present, meaning phone turned off, paying attention to whoever is talking.

▪ Avoid criticizing and blaming. Again, if things get heated, call a time-out.

There are several questions you must ask yourself before the conversation starts. Write down your answers, which will form the basis of the script you'll use. You can memorize it, like an actor remembering lines. Or you can carry it with you and read from it. This second approach is especially good if you've never initiated a conversation with your parents, or if you expect it to be awkward and difficult. It might seem strange to read from a script, but it shows a couple of things that are important to communicate. First, you're a little nervous, and that's okay. Second, you're taking this seriously. You've thought about it and prepared. That's good work on your part.

THE QUESTIONS

What do you want to talk about? What's on your mind? What do you want to ask, tell, explain, or discuss?

What do you want from the conversation? This is different from the bigger question of what you want to change about your relationship with your parents. Remember the strategy we discussed earlier about managing the situation and not the relationship? This is the same thing, only the situation happens to be a conversation. You might want your parents to listen and not interrupt or give advice. Or maybe you want them to share their opinion. Maybe you need help problem-solving something. Maybe you want to have an exchange of ideas. Maybe you want to be understood, or have your emotions validated. Maybe you want permission to go to a party or plan a trip. Be as specific as you can.

What do you *not* want from the conversation? Think of possible responses or outcomes that would upset you. Examples include lectures, unwanted advice, criticism and judgment, anger, too many questions, your parents sharing parts of the conversation with others, being dismissed or not believed, etc.

How do you feel about having a conversation with your parents on this topic? Fear, nervousness, apathy, cynicism, weariness? If you're having trouble connecting to your emotions, go back to the section titled "Your Emotional Blueprint", which begins on page 74, and find the checklist. Read through all the items you checked. See if any of them resonate. If there are too many, ask yourself, "If I could only pick one of these to represent my deepest feelings about this conversation, which would it be?"

What is the best outcome for the conversation? What would it look like if it goes well and you get exactly what you need?

What is the worst outcome for this conversation? Might your parents get defensive and angry? Might they joke around when you need them to be serious? Get distracted? Focus on themselves and their issues? Write down how they might respond. What exactly do you think they'll say? How will they say it? If you can, write it out word for word, including descriptions of body language, facial expressions, etc. (If you're struggling to come up with anything, go back to the section titled "Parent Problems" on page 46).

What might you do to help your parents through the conversation? If you're wondering why it's your job to help them, consider this: The goal here is to maximize your chances of getting what you want from the situation. For example, if your parents are prone to getting defensive and even a little paranoid, you might say, "Can we talk for two minutes? I need to go over something with you, but don't worry: It's just about lacrosse signups." Or, in the case of an overinvolved parent who can't help giving instructions, say, "I'm having a tough time with something. I want to tell you about it, and I need you to listen. I don't need suggestions or a plan."

Your answers to these questions should inform

the script you come up with. Or you can use the samples below and add in whatever is relevant to your situation.

SAMPLE SCRIPTS

Below are three scripts of typical conversations that end badly, meaning that both parent and teen walk away feeling angry, frustrated, or hurt. Each scenario will be presented in three parts. The first part, or *Script*, shows the dialogue of the teen and parent struggling to communicate effectively. The second part, or *Discussion*, examines why the conversation isn't working. The last part, *Rewrite*, shows a new and improved script and lets you see the positive impact of the changes.

CONVERSATION ABOUT YOUR MENTAL HEALTH

Teen:

"Mom, I need to talk with you about something. I've been feeling really depressed. It's been getting in the way of my life because on some days I can't get out of bed, and I'm having trouble keeping up in school. But the biggest problem is I just feel sad. I don't even want to do the things that used to be fun. I've been afraid to tell you because I know you're stressed with work and the divorce, but I really need some help."

Parent's reaction:

Let's say that the mom is the uninvolved parent type, but she's also prone to defensiveness and using guilt trips whenever she's questioned. What this looks like on a day-to-day basis is that she takes care of the essentials like going to work, grocery shopping, and giving her kids rides when asked. But aside from those things, she's not involved.

Case in point, when her teen started isolating, sleeping too much, and neglecting their hygiene, she didn't notice. Her response to the above conversation? She takes a deep breath and says, "I don't know what you want me to do. I'm stretched so thin right now and you're going to blame me because my job is hard? Because I'm divorcing your father? What do you want, for me to stay married to someone who drinks and cheats on me? Is that what you want?"

Where did the teen's script go wrong? Overall, it's pretty good, but it doesn't consider the mom's difficulty connecting on an emotional level. She doesn't know how to handle it, especially the open-ended request for help. Her response is predictably defensive. She's basically saying "What do you want from me? What am I supposed to do?" She's also personalizing her teen's depression. She's seeing it as a reflection of her poor parenting and her decision to get divorced.

What's needed, then, is a smaller, more concrete ask. It has to fit with the mom's limited abilities. Let's rewrite it.

Rewrite

"Mom, I need to talk with you about something, and I just need you to listen. I've been feeling really depressed and I'm having trouble getting out of bed and keeping up in school. I know you've got a lot on your plate right now, but I thought you should know what's going on with me."

The important changes are 1) it's shorter, 2) the need for her to listen is stated clearly and up front, and 3) the ask at the end of the script is limited to having the mom know what's going on with her teen. You might be wondering, "Doesn't this teen need more from the mom than just awareness?" Yes, definitely. But, because of the mom's defensiveness, it's helpful to split it up into two conversations. The first is to let her know that her teen is depressed. The second would address the problem-solving piece.

CONVERSATION TO ADDRESS A PARENT'S BEHAVIOR

Teen:

"Dad, I need to get something off my chest. A few days ago, when you said I couldn't hold a job because I don't like to work hard, it really hurt. I didn't lose that job because of anything I did. The store closed. And I got a new job two weeks later. But what I really want to say is this: Remember when we used to do stuff together, like going fishing, and taking the dogs to the lake? I miss doing those things. What do you think about doing something this weekend?"

Parent:

"Honestly, I don't even remember saying that. I

must have been joking. And admit it: You hated that job. You complained about it all the time."

Teen:

"Even if you were joking, it still hurt, which is why I'm telling you. I want us to get along better. I miss that."

Parent:

"Okay. I'll try and be more careful about what I say. And about the other thing, sure. Let's plan on going fishing this weekend."

Discussion

What's great about the son's script is that he stated what happened and how it made him feel. He could have asked for his father to stop criticizing, but that might not have gone over so well. I imagine the father responding "Don't be so sensitive." Instead, the son shifted to talking about his desire to do an activity together. It's an especially effective transition because a) he's asking his father to do something fun that they used to enjoy together, and b) he's linking the criticizing behavior to the lack of connection in their relationship. The father may not pick up on this, but it doesn't matter. The message is clear: Be more thoughtful so they can enjoy each other's company the way they used to.

CONVERSATION ABOUT EVERYDAY THINGS

Teen: "Hey, how was your day?"

Parent (looking at teen suspiciously): "Wait. What's going on?"

Teen: "Nothing."

Parent: "You never ask about my day. You must want something. What is it, money, to borrow the car? Or maybe you're in trouble."

Teen: "Why do you always assume I'm in trouble?"

Parent: "Because you usually are. I'm still getting robocalls from the school, by the way, about you skipping seventh period. Every day. Where are you going? I'll bet you're vaping with that Sheedy boy."

Teen (turning to leave): "I can't talk to you. What's the point?"

Discussion

This is a typical bad script because both parties are locked into negative responses that don't serve either of them. No one gets what they want. It starts to go off the rails after the parent says "What do you want?" Instead of saying "To talk to you," or "To have a conversation," the teen responds with his own accusation. "Why do you think I'm in trouble?" Which is to say, why do you always assume the worst? Why don't you trust me?

From there it spirals the rest of the way down the drain. The real problem here is that the parent and teen are locked into a model of communicating that is based on sarcasm and mistrust. Let's turn it around and fix it. I'm going to give this teen the gift of a sense of humor. Watch how he uses it.

Rewrite

Teen: "Hey, how was your day?"

Parent (looking at teen suspiciously): "Wait. What's going on?"

Teen: "Nothing."

Parent: "You never ask about my day. You must want something. What is it, money, to borrow the car? Or maybe you're in trouble."

Teen (smiling): "Nope. Not in trouble. Don't need the car. Money's always good, though. But seriously, I'm just trying to have a regular, everyday conversation with my mom. You know the kind: You tell me about your day, and then I'll tell you about mine. Isn't that what regular people do?"

Parent (smiling too): "Are you accusing me of being a regular person?" (Laughs.) "Well, it was a crappy day, if you want to know the truth. I've got this coworker who's really tough to deal with. She was supposed to finish this productivity report, but of course she—" (Notices teen's eyes glazing over.) "Anyway, how was your day?"

Teen: (looking more alive): "Glad you asked. I had an awesome day. First, we got our math tests back. I'd been worried about my grade because it was on this factorial stuff that makes no sense. But I studied a lot, and guess what . . ."

Discussion

This one is much better. Did you observe the point of change? It's when, instead of accusing, the teen responds with a joke. It lets the parent know that the conversation is supposed to be lighthearted and nothing is being asked other than to play along. Some parents might not be able to do this, but many can. Remember, it's just a few minutes. A short exchange like this isn't going to alter anyone's personality or fix the relationship, but it's a start. It's something to build on.

CHECK-IN

"If you're not ready to start a conversation with your parents, that's okay. Focus on non-talking strategies. Or work on a script for a future conversation. The important thing is to trust your instincts and move forward when it feels right. And if you try but it goes badly, that's okay, too. It doesn't mean that you did it wrong. Changing how you and your parents talk to each other is hard work; it's going to take time."

BEYOND YOUR PARENTS

At some point you're going to leave your parents. Maybe you're heading off to college or finding a job and your own apartment. Or joining the military, traveling, or something else. Maybe you've got several more years at home but are starting to think ahead. Whatever the circumstances, there will come a time when you need to begin meeting some of your emotional needs outside of your family. This is totally normal, but it's a challenging process, even in the best of circumstances. When you have problem parents, it's infinitely more difficult, because they aren't likely to notice or respond to your changing needs. Or they will, but not in the right way.

The last part of the book will focus on the skills and

strategies you'll need to form relationships outside of your family, with friends, roommates, coworkers, partners, and others. These skills will help you:

- Find well-adjusted people

- Avoid toxic people

- Recognize old patterns and stop yourself from repeating the pain of the past

- Be yourself and trust your own instincts

- Say no without feeling guilty or selfish

- Make mistakes without self-judgment

- Experience joy

HOW TO FIND WELL-ADJUSTED PEOPLE

If you've grown up with problem parents, you've probably gotten used to bad behaviors. You may even see them as normal, or "not a big deal." This can carry over into non-family relationships with predictably negative results: You end up focusing more on the needs of others than on your own. But do you want to? Do you want to keep putting other people's needs ahead of your own? I'm hoping at this point you're going to respond with a resounding no. A "hell no." I'm hoping you're enough of an expert now to see that doing this strips you of your self-esteem and pushes you away from your true self.

But the question remains: How do you find people who are pleasant to be around and will treat you well? What do they look like? Where do they hang out? Is there a special handshake you can use to distinguish them? Here are some defining characteristics of people who are safe to have as friends and partners:

- They're easygoing.

- They know how to have fun.

- They're supportive and helpful.

- They can tolerate stress, occasional bad news, and ups and downs in their life. This doesn't mean they don't ever get upset or sad. They do, but they handle it.

- They don't need to be the center of attention.

- They don't lie.

- They know how to say "I'm sorry" in a real and genuine way.

- They thank you when you're polite or do something nice for them.

- They pay you back when they borrow money. If you're driving, they offer to help pay for gas. If you loan them clothing or something else, you get it back.

- They return favors and gestures. If you get them a birthday present, they do the same when it's your birthday.

- They recognize social cues and boundaries and respect them. If you point one out, they get it and don't need you to spell it out and explain.

- They can manage their own emotions.

- They're able to change their mind and admit they're wrong.

- They're responsible and (reasonably) punctual.

It may feel weird to be around happy, supportive people. You may have gotten used to sarcasm and insults as a stand-in for closeness. Maybe you're not quite sure how to respond to kindness. This is okay. Let it be weird. When you're around new people, ask yourself these questions:

- "Do I feel safe to be myself around this person?"

- "Does it feel like I can relax?"

• "Can I let my guard down and not be on the lookout for criticism or judgment?"

If the answers to these questions are skewing in the right direction, then go with it. And as a final test, if you're still unsure, ask yourself this question: Do you feel that this person sees, hears, and understands you?

HOW TO AVOID TOXIC PEOPLE

Okay, you know how to find good people, but what about toxic people who may seem magnetically drawn to you? Why is it that you seem to attract needy people? Why do your friends use you for emotional support without ever giving anything back?

If this seems true for you, it's likely that you are emotionally sensitive and they are not. You are aware of your friends' emotions, and you respond appropriately. They, however, have no clue about *your* emotions. If you're hurt or upset, they're not going to notice. And if they say something insensitive or hurtful and you call them on it, you're likely to hear back:

- "What's your problem, dude?"

- "What? I was just kidding."

- "Sensitive much? Get over yourself."

- "Lighten up."

- "You're way too uptight/touchy/fragile."

- "Don't be such a drama queen."

- "You take yourself way too seriously."

- "Why don't you call me when you
grow up."

There are *behaviors* that are tipoffs too. If you see any of the following, you may want to rethink your friendship:

- They only call or text when they're in
distress and need support (or money, or a ride,
or to borrow something).

- They're unreliable, forgetting plans or showing up really late and not understanding why it's a problem.

- They don't return favors or pay back loans.

- They don't reciprocate invitations and gifts, or even return texts.

- They can't say they're sorry, even when they're obviously at fault (though they may be able to half apologize, as in, "I'm sorry you're mad," or "I know things didn't turn out so good").

- They need to be the center of attention.

- They don't say thank you and seem generally entitled.

- They play the victim.

- They have a strong need for drama. If they can't find any, they'll create it.

- They only have time for you after a breakup or when no one more popular is available.

Keep in mind that sometimes people who are poor choices as friends or partners can seem really together at first. They might be smart, funny, and charismatic. They might have lots of free time and like doing similar things. They might be successful in school or activities. But when you get to know them better, the relationship begins to feel increasingly unbalanced.

If you're unsure, don't get into a game of pros and cons. Just ask yourself: "What do I get back from this friendship?" It's not that friendships are all about rewards, but you should be able to come up with a few examples of what your friend brings to the relationship table. If it's little more than attention and availability, think twice. Do you need more than that from a friend? Absolutely.

If you're already in a one-sided friendship, you can use the tools and strategies you've learned in this book to make it better. But ask yourself first, "Do I have the energy to devote to this task? Do I want to?" and "Can I be in this friendship without compromising my sense of who I am?" Let the answer to this last question be your ultimate guide.

RECOGNIZING (AND BREAKING) PATTERNS

There will come a time when you find yourself repeating old patterns. Let's say it's something you worked hard to change, like not making excuses for your parents' behavior. You've made progress but you catch yourself doing it again. This can be upsetting and bring up all kinds of fears. Maybe things haven't changed at all. Maybe things will never change. Maybe all your hard work has been for nothing.

When old behaviors and patterns reemerge, notice it, but don't judge. It's not failure. It's normal. Say to yourself, "I'm doing it again. Interesting." Ask yourself if any changes or triggers have occurred. If so, note that too.

If there have been no changes or triggers, no stress or conflict, it's okay. People are creatures of habit and may take comfort in even the most unpleasant behaviors. It's familiar. Predictable. The reasons for this are too complicated to go into here.

Just know that the process for breaking a pattern is straightforward:

Observe the behavior. You can do this yourself, as long as you have a way to notice in the first place. Some people can set a filter in their mind to catch it when it occurs. Others tell a trusted friend or sibling and recruit them to help. Say, for example, you're withdrawing. In this case, your friend would pull you aside and say, "Remember when you asked me to let you know when . . . ?" You might say, "Oh, I'm doing it again? Thanks. I appreciate it."

Label the behavior. You should be getting the hang of this step by now. Simply call it what it is. "I'm walking on eggshells." "I'm making excuses for my parents." "I'm avoiding them."

Shift to a different response or activity. Make something to eat. Do something active, like taking a walk. Listen to music. Have a conversation. It doesn't matter, as long as it interrupts the old pattern.

STAYING TRUE TO YOURSELF

When you've grown up with problem parents, it can be hard to stay true to yourself. This often shows up as a fear of making mistakes, difficulty saying no to others, or an inability to trust your instincts. Becoming disconnected from yourself can affect your mood, self-esteem, and even your ability to make decisions.

It may seem obvious, but you should feel free to be exactly who you are. This means having your own thoughts, feelings, interests, tastes, opinions, and political views. You should be free to like who you want and also to dislike who you want. You should be free to feel a certain way (happy, sad, angry) even if others want you to feel differently. The following are skills you can practice to reconnect with yourself. You might be tempted to try them all at once, but there's no need to rush. You have the rest of your life.

MAKING MISTAKES

Give yourself the freedom to make mistakes. If you have demanding, controlling parents, you may have grown up in near-constant fear of doing something wrong. Maybe you were punished or criticized when you made mistakes. You may have been judged as incompetent or bad.

If you have parents who are overprotective or micromanage your life, you may have learned to approach challenges—even normal, necessary ones—with a great deal of fear and anxiety. You've heard too many lectures about safety, or the need to hit all your marks in the right order, every time. The result of these kinds of messages is to avoid challenges because failure is unacceptable. Actually, what's unacceptable is the idea of going through life in near-constant fear of making mistakes and bad decisions. Mistakes are a normal part of learning. You deserve to be free to try new things, occasionally fail, and learn from your mistakes. How? Try the following:

- Challenge yourself from time to time. It could be something new, or something familiar but with a twist.

- Reframe failure and mistakes as feedback. It's just information; it doesn't have to mean anything about who you are as a person.

- If your parents have a hard time with your

mistakes, try your best to disconnect and let that be their problem. You're just being a healthy teen who is learning about life; they're the ones hung up on fear and perfectionism. And guess what? They have the rest of their lives to work on it. You, however, will be making much better use of your time enjoying your life.

SETTING YOUR OWN GOALS

Practice setting your own goals, even if they're bad ones! This doesn't mean that your parents can't ever offer guidance or try to protect you from harm. That's parenting, and even if your parents are bad at some aspects of it, you're still going to need guidance and support. What I mean here is, have any goal you want, so long as it's meaningful to you. If you want to be a Marine and your parents are pacifists, Semper Fi! They can disagree, but it's still your goal. If you dream of going to private college in New England, but your parents can only afford state college tuition, it can still be your goal. You may have to do a lot of extra work to get there, but that's for you to figure out.

- Make sure your goals are yours and not overly influenced by others.

- Commit to doing the work needed to make progress on your goals.

- If you find that your goals no longer serve you, change them.

SAYING NO

Growing up with problem parents often leads to a tendency to put others' needs before your own. This shows up most clearly as an inability to say no. But now, knowing what you do about setting boundaries and other skills, you should feel free to use the most powerful two-letter word in English. *No*. It takes commitment and practice, but the following will get you started:

- Recognize when you're being asked or pressured to do something you don't want to do.

- Say no without offering an explanation or justification.

- Observe how you feel and own it.

TRUSTING YOUR INSTINCTS

If you're used to second-guessing yourself or explaining away what you really want, it can be extremely hard to trust your instincts. This skill may take the longest to develop, so be patient and keep at it.

- If you're alone—or you're not, but you don't especially care what others think—cover your heart with your right hand and close your eyes. Ask yourself: "What am I really thinking and feeling right now? What's best for me in this situation?"

- Think about a time when you made a decision and were 100 percent certain it was the right choice. What did that feel like? Try to connect with the physical sensations as well as thoughts and emotions.

Write it down here: _____

_____

_____

_____

_____

_____

_____

Think back to a time when you made the wrong decision but convinced yourself it was okay. In other words, you acted against your own instincts. What did that feel like? Connect to the sensations, thoughts, and emotions. Write it down here: _____

_____

_____

_____

_____

_____

_____

SEEKING JOY

Depending on your circumstances, you may have to scroll back very far in the film reel of your life to find a moment of joy. For some teens it's recent enough. "I went to a concert with my friends. The band was awesome, and I danced the whole time and didn't think for a minute about my problems."

For other teens the experience of joy is a fading, distant memory. "I remember in the fifth grade getting a new Lego expert kit. I was happy for weeks, putting it together using the instructions, and then taking it apart and seeing what else I could build from the pieces." And sometimes it predates the death of someone close. "It was in middle school, before my grandmother passed. She used to live with us and we'd bake cookies and watch TV."

Even if it's been a long time since you've felt joy, it's not too late. The trick is to go about it with gentleness and patience. What does that mean? Imagine trying to tame a feral cat. If you walked over to it and tried to pick it up, it would disappear into the woods. But if you leave a little food in a dish, at the edge of the tree line, it might come closer.

Repeat. Eventually, the cat might come close enough to brush against your legs. Finding joy after you've been stressed and unhappy can be very similar. If your bullshit meter is still twitching away, read through the responsibilities below and then decide.

Open yourself to the possibility of joy. Maybe you don't think you'll ever feel it again, but can you believe that it's possible? Even if you can't, try saying this out loud when no one is around: "I'm opening myself to the *possibility* of finding joy in my life. I want to be happy and have fun, and it's okay right now if I don't really know how."

Surround yourself with positive people. Notice I didn't say happy people. The reasons are twofold. First, if you're really stressed and unhappy, it can be overwhelming to be around happy people. Second, *happy* and *positive* aren't always the same thing. Positive people are pleasant to be around. They're balanced, and forward moving. They have tough times like everyone else, but they deal with them in a way that doesn't interfere with their outlook on life.

You can gain a lot from being around positive people. It feels good to spend time with them. They make excellent friends and partners. And you can observe them up close and personal to see how they do it.

Be present once per day. This means tuning in to your surroundings, and bringing your full awareness and presence to the moment. Make it deliberate. Say, "Okay, right now I'm going to be fully present in this moment. I will let go of my fears and worries, and will be open to whatever this moment has to offer." The moment can be anything: sitting with your dog or cat, listening to music, going out in the sun or the cold, whatever. Pay attention to your senses. Notice sounds, colors, textures, and smells. Resist the urge to categorize, judge, or even interpret what's happening. As much as you're able, just be in the moment and experience it fully.

Become curious. If you'll allow me to make a big statement without any proof whatsoever, curiosity is the overlooked superpower of our time. There's so much talk about IQ (intelligence quotient), EQ (emotional intelligence quotient), and even things like bodily-kinesthetic intelligence and musical-rhythmic intelligence. But for me, curiosity rules them all.

If I believed strongly in the concept of intelligence

as a real thing that can be measured—which I don't—I'd call it CQ, for Curiosity Quotient. Instead, I'll tell you what you need to know about curiosity, especially as it relates to finding joy. First, as life stress increases, curiosity diminishes. In cases of extreme stress, it goes away completely. This makes total sense when you think about a person's needs in crisis situations. The need to survive the crisis eclipses all other needs.

So how to turn the curiosity switch back on? If you already have a hobby or interest, dive right in, but do so in a slightly different way. Better yet, come up with a question. Let's say you make pottery. You might ask, "I wonder what would happen if instead of doing it this way, I..."

If you don't have any hobbies or interests, pick a time when you're around other people, driving to school, walking the halls, etc. Say to yourself, "Okay, now I'm going to look for something interesting. I don't know what it's going to be, but I'm going to keep my eyes peeled." I guarantee something will come up. Why? Because your brain is wired to look for patterns and try to keep you safe. It responds to new and interesting things, but it's not very good at searching for them. Still, it can do this, and it's a skill you can cultivate and get better at. To take it up a notch, keep a notebook (or use a notes app in your phone) and record the interesting things you see. Then, on days when you're too tired to search for something interesting, you can simply look back at your list and enjoy your past observations.

THE END
IS NOT
THE END

I hope this book has helped you. I hope it's clear that the problems that led you here have nothing to do with personal flaws or shortcomings. There's nothing wrong with you. You're not broken, and you don't need to be fixed. You are worthy of being loved, and you do not need to put your parents' feelings ahead of your own.

What's wrong is a lack of emotional connection— at home and in the world around you. What's needed is information (about why your parents aren't recognizing and responding to your emotional needs) and a new set of tools (to help you build connection and get more of your needs met).

In our time together we've covered a lot of

information and learned how to use many tools. Now it's time for you to try them out. When you do, pay close attention to the ones that work best for you and your situation. It's okay if you use only a couple and forget the rest. Just keep practicing. Observe the results and make adjustments. And then practice more. This is how we grow.

In time, maybe you and your parents will be closer. Maybe they will stop saying hurtful things and trying to control your life. Or maybe they will still do those things, but it won't affect you as much because you know how to set boundaries and can see yourself as a separate person. Whatever the case, you're learning how to work with reality and meet your needs. You're learning to be yourself. This is amazing, and I couldn't be happier for you.

But please don't stop here. Think of this book as a gate you're opening. Beyond the gate lies possibility: the possibility of becoming closer to your parents. Of being seen and heard by them. Of being understood. The possibility that this connection will continue to grow and deepen throughout your life. Until you feel safe. Until you feel that you truly belong.

And then? Then you can do anything. Once you've learned to understand and accept your feelings and be yourself, you get to enjoy the ultimate freedom: to choose exactly how you want to live.

RESOURCES

Below is a list of resources that might be helpful on your journey of healing and self-discovery. Feel free to explore on your own, too, as there will be many new books, websites, and apps in the next few years. And remember: Seeking knowledge and understanding, and asking for help when needed, are always good things to do!

HOTLINES

988 Suicide & Crisis Lifeline: If you or someone you know is struggling or in crisis, call or text 988 or chat at 988lifeline.org. The 988 Suicide & Crisis Lifeline is a national network of local crisis centers that provides free and confidential emotional support to people in suicidal crisis or emotional distress 24 hours a day, 7 days a week.

Crisis Text Line: Text from anywhere anytime to talk to a trained Crisis Counselor. Text HOME to 74741.

National Child Abuse Hotline: For confidential crisis intervention, information, and referrals, call 1-800-4-A-CHILD (1-800-422-4453).

The National Sexual Assault Telephone Hotline: To be connected with a trained staff member from a sexual assault service provider in your area, call 800-656-HOPE (4673).

The Trevor Project: Provides a safe, confidential place for LGBTQ+ youth to get support. Call 866-488-7386 or text START to 678678.

APPS

Calm (calm.com): Features meditation, sleep stories, and breathing exercises to help with relaxation and stress management.

Headspace (headspace.com): Offers guided meditation and mindfulness exercises to reduce stress and improve overall well-being.

NotOK (notokapp.com): A pre-crisis tool developed

by teens that provides a single-click message to your trusted contacts.

Oak (oakmeditation.com): A free meditation and breathing app that is easy to use.

ORGANIZATIONS

Covenant House (covenanthouse.org/homeless -shelters): Provides housing and supportive services to youth dealing with homelessness.

Go Ask Alice! (goaskalice.columbia.edu): Q&A focusing on emotional health, supported by a team from Columbia University.

Jed Foundation (jedfoundation.org): Protects emotional health and prevents suicide for teens and young adults.

Love is Respect: Offers extensive information on healthy relationships and signs of abuse. Chat at loveisrespect.org or text LOVEIS to 866-331-9474.

Mental Health America (mhanational.org): MHA is a national nonprofit dedicated to promoting mental health and well-being. Their website is comprehensive and loaded with great resources for teens.